THE WHICH? GUIDE TO
RENTING AND LETTING

About the author

Peter Wilde is a practising solicitor in north-west England, specialising in landlord and tenant law. He is also a visiting lecturer at the College of Law, Chester.

Thanks are also due to Diane Campbell, author of the chapters on renting and letting practices in Scotland; a practising solicitor, she is currently the legal manager at Strathkelvin District Council.

THE WHICH? GUIDE TO
RENTING
AND LETTING

PETER WILDE

CONSUMERS' ASSOCIATION

Which? Books are commissioned and researched by
The Association for Consumer Research
and published by Consumers' Association,
2 Marylebone Road, London NW1 4DF

Distributed by The Penguin Group:
Penguin Books Ltd, 27 Wrights Lane, London W8 5TZ

First edition June 1994
Copyright © 1994 Consumers' Association Ltd

British Library Cataloguing in Publication Data
Wilde, Peter
    Which? Guide to Renting and Letting. –
(Which? Consumer Guides)
    I. Title II. Series
    333.5

ISBN 0 85202 520 3

The author would like to thank Paul Butt, a principal lecturer at the College
of Law, Chester for his kind assistance in the preparation of this book.

Typographic design by Paul Saunders

Cover photographs courtesy of ACE/Mark French, The Geoffrey Goode
Picture Collection, Bubbles/Jacqui Farrow

Typeset by J&L Composition Ltd, Filey, North Yorkshire

Printed and bound by
Firmin-Didot (France), Group Herissey,
No d'impression: 26937

CONTENTS

Throughout this book for 'he' read 'he or she'

INTRODUCTION

YOU may be a potential landlord thinking of letting a house, flat or bedsitting room. You may have already done so but find you need to know your legal position. Or perhaps you are a tenant, wanting to know where you stand in a dispute with your landlord. The law of landlord and tenant is complex: it is a mixture of ancient common law (judge-made law), numerous Acts of Parliament and regulations made over many years, frequently subject to change. This book is no substitute for obtaining professional legal advice, but explains what the law is and how it is normally interpreted in practice.

The type of questions often asked include:

- which is the best way of letting a house or a flat?
- is there any control over the amount of rent that can be charged?
- who is liable for repairs?
- who pays the council tax, the water rates and the gas and electricity bills?
- can the tenant be evicted when the tenancy ends?
- what is the correct procedure for repossessing tenanted property?
- what is the tenant's position if the landlord tries to harass him into leaving or tries to evict him without a court order?
- if a Rent Act tenant is evicted will he be rehoused by the local authority?
- can the landlord demand a deposit against breakages or rent arrears?

- what protection is there for council tenants or tenants of housing associations?
- does the tenant have the right to buy the freehold of the flat he rents?

These are just a few of the issues addressed in this book. However, before taking an in-depth look at the detailed rules which govern the law of landlord and tenant, it is worth looking at some of the unfortunate situations which can arise when things go wrong.

The assured shorthold tenancy that wasn't

Mr and Mrs A were the owners of a flat which they intended to let on a six-month assured shorthold tenancy. They bought from a law stationer a printed form of agreement and the prescribed form of notice which they knew had to be given to the tenant before the agreement was signed. The agreement was duly signed on 2 April 1993 and the tenant moved in. However, unbenown to Mr and Mrs A, the prescribed form of notice had been changed on 1 April 1993, making the assured shorthold tenancy invalid. At the end of the six-month period the tenant claimed that he had full security of tenure and refused to move out. The courts had no power to dispute his claim and Mr and Mrs A were left with a tenant they could not move. The situation became even more worrying for Mr and Mrs A when the tenant married a few months later. Not only was the tenant entitled to remain in their flat until his death, but his wife could then take over the tenancy and remain there for the duration of her lifetime as well. Because of one simple error, what Mr and Mrs A had intended to be a six-month arrangement was set to last for the foreseeable future.

The resident landlord who moved out

Mrs B owned a large house which had been converted into two flats. She lived in the ground-floor flat and let the first-floor flat to a tenant on a monthly tenancy. Because she was a resident landlord, she was able to create a tenancy which gave the tenant very little statutory protection. Mrs B eventually had to move to a retirement home, and she died three years later; the tenant remained in occupation throughout, always paying his rent in full and on time. Mrs B's executors wanted vacant possession of the house for sale and gave the tenant notice to quit. However, because the landlord must be resident at both the start of the tenancy *and* at its termination for the resident landlord rules to apply, the tenant was quite within his rights when he refused to move out. He had become a fully protected tenant and was now entitled to live in the house for the rest of his life. The executors could evict the tenant only if they could prove a ground for possession such as rent arrears, not available in this case. Furthermore, if the tenant were to die leaving a spouse, the spouse could then take over the property until his or her death.

The unwelcome subtenant

Mr C let his flat only to discover after a few months that the original tenant had sublet the property to someone else. He had no power to check the subtenant's references and when he tried to terminate the tenancy found that the subtenant could claim security of tenure against him. These problems could have been avoided if Mr C had inserted a clause in the original tenancy agreement *forbidding* the tenant to sublet without his consent. Because of the absence of this vital clause, Mr C was saddled with a tenant he did not want and whom he could not evict.

The unexpected repair bill

Mr and Mrs D let their house on a weekly tenancy, unaware that the roof was in dire need of repair. However, the tenants quickly noticed the problem and insisted that it was put right without delay. Mr and Mrs D's plea that they did not have the money to do the repairs was to no avail. They discovered that in most short-term tenancies (i.e. those of less than seven years), the landlord is obliged to repair the structure and exterior of the property, no matter how costly this may be. They also discovered that a landlord can be prosecuted for disrepair and that, in certain circumstances, if the landlord fails to do the repairs for which he is liable, the tenant can get the work done himself and recover the cost by withholding rent.

The landlord who didn't inform his mortgage lender
Mrs E let her flat but never informed the building society with whom the flat was mortgaged of this arrangement. When she got into financial difficulties, the tenant was shocked to realise that the building society intended to repossess the property and evict him, despite the fact that he had signed a tenancy agreement, always paid his rent on time and had known nothing about the mortgage. The tenant had not realised that all prospective tenants of private landlords ought to ascertain whether or not there is a mortgage on the property.

As this book will show, most of these problems are avoidable. Time and money can be saved, and in some cases costly legal action avoided, if both landlord and tenant are aware of the laws that govern the various types of tenancy, and how they are applied in practice.

This book explains the law and procedure in England and Wales, and briefly outlines the main differences which apply in Scotland.

CHAPTER 1

WHAT IS A TENANCY?

A TENANCY is an arrangement under which exclusive possession of a property is granted for a fixed or ascertainable period of time. It is, of course, usually granted in return for rent but rent is not, legally, an essential part of a tenancy (although landlords who do not charge rent are few and far between). A lease is exactly the same as a tenancy, although in practice the expression 'lease' usually indicates that the property is let for a *fixed* term, e.g. six months or a specified number of years, whereas a tenancy usually indicates a *periodic* letting, e.g. where property is let from week to week or from month to month until terminated by notice. However, the key requirements of any lease or tenancy are:

- a letting for a 'fixed or ascertainable period of time'
- the granting of 'exclusive possession'.

Fixed or ascertainable period

A tenancy or lease must be granted for a period which is defined from the outset or which is capable of being made certain by the act of either party. This presents no difficulty in the vast majority of cases. The tenancy agreement or lease will stipulate when the tenancy is to commence and when (or how) it is to end. The duration of the term is thus known or ascertainable from the outset. Sometimes, however, the situation is less clear. A recent case involving land adjoining a highway concerned a lease which was granted 'until the land was required for road-widening purposes'. It was held that the land could not be leased for this indefinite period of time as no one could say in advance when the land would be required for this purpose: a 'fixed' or 'ascertainable' period could not therefore be set.

In the case of periodic lettings, although the letting is for an indefinite period, the requirement of certainty is still satisfied. The distinction is that although the tenancy may be allowed to carry on indefinitely, either party may terminate by giving a notice to quit which expires at the end of a relevant week or month of that tenancy. The only uncertainty is *when* the landlord or tenant will choose to give notice; the termination of the letting is not an uncertain duration, dependent upon some future or uncertain event, but can be made certain by either landlord or tenant.

Exclusive possession

Exclusive possession of the property or a defined part of it needs to be specifically granted to the tenant. If the occupier is merely given the right to *share* occupation, e.g. with the owner, but not given the *exclusive* use of a specific part of the property, the arrangement would amount to a licence, not a lease or a tenancy. This point is very important since tenants have substantial statutory protection (e.g. under the Rent Acts and Housing Acts) which does not, generally, apply to licensees. This point is considered in more detail on page 67. A lodger who merely shares a house with the owner, where the owner has unrestricted access to the lodger's bedroom for cleaning, providing bed linen or services, is usually regarded as a licensee with very little protection under the law. If the owner dies, or sells the house to someone else, the lodger's rights (which are merely personal rights of occupation) would not be binding against the owner's successor. A tenant, on the other hand, is regarded as having an 'interest' in the property, which can be binding on the landlord's successor. Although this book is primarily concerned with the rights of landlords and tenants rather than licensors and licensees, residential licences will be covered where appropriate.

Statutory controls

Despite what may have been agreed in the tenancy agreement or lease, many tenants are protected by Acts of Parliament

Chart 1: Public sector tenancies

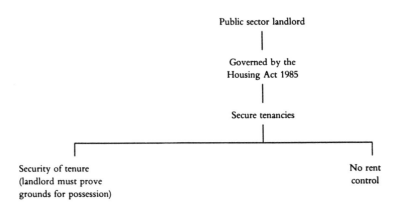

Public sector landlord

Governed by the
Housing Act 1985

Secure tenancies

Security of tenure
(landlord must prove
grounds for possession)

No rent
control

Chart 2: Private sector tenancies

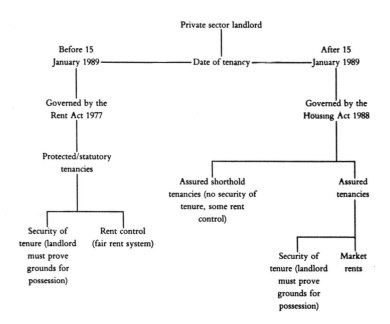

Private sector landlord

Before 15
January 1989 ——————— Date of tenancy ——————— After 15
January 1989

Governed by the
Rent Act 1977

Governed by the
Housing Act 1988

Protected/statutory
tenancies

Assured shorthold
tenancies (no security of
tenure, some rent
control)

Assured
tenancies

Security of
tenure (landlord
must prove
grounds for
possession)

Rent control
(fair rent system)

Security of
tenure (landlord
must prove
grounds for
possession)

Market
rents

7

Chart 3: Housing association tenancies

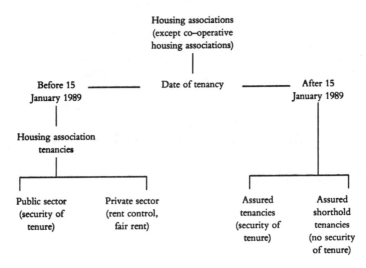

and statutory regulations. Even if the landlord terminates the tenancy by proper methods this does not always mean that the tenant has to leave. Some Acts of Parliament give the tenant the right to continue in residence despite the termination of the tenancy agreement. Similarly, the rent which the landlord and the tenant have agreed in the tenancy agreement is not always the rent that can lawfully be recovered.

In deciding which of these statutory provisions apply, a distinction must be made between public and private sector tenancies. The vast majority of local authority lettings (and certain others in the public sector) are known as 'secure' tenancies and are governed by the Housing Act 1985 (see Chart 1). Secure tenants, in the main, enjoy substantial security of tenure but with very little statutory control over the amount of rent that can be charged. On the other hand, most tenancies in the private sector are governed either by the Rent Act 1977 or the Housing Act 1988 (see Chart 2). Private sector tenancies granted prior to 15 January 1989 usually fall within the Rent Act 1977 and are known as either 'protected' tenancies or 'statutory' tenancies. Protected or statutory tenants enjoy substantial security of tenure *and* a significant degree of control over the amount of rent that the landlord can charge. Where a private landlord granted a tenancy on or after 15 January 1989 he is usually governed by the terms of the Housing Act 1988. Under this Act the tenancy may either be an 'assured' tenancy or an 'assured shorthold' tenancy. Under an assured tenancy the tenant has substantial security of tenure but there is little statutory control over the amount of rent that the landlord can charge. If the tenancy is an assured shorthold tenancy (which must be for a minimum of six months) the tenant has no security of tenure once the fixed term has come to an end but he is given some degree of protection against 'excessive' rents being charged.

Tenancies granted by housing associations are, in the main, treated as if they were in the public sector if they were granted prior to 15 January 1989, but as private sector tenancies if granted on or after that date (see Chart 3).

CHAPTER 2

ASSURED TENANCIES

'ASSURED tenancy' is the name given by the 1988 Housing Act to lettings in the private sector which fulfil certain conditions. These conditions are discussed later, but for the moment it can be assumed that, unless special circumstances exist, any tenancy entered into on or after 15 January 1989 is likely to be an assured tenancy – and remember, a tenancy can be validly created by word of mouth; a written agreement is not essential.

If an assured tenancy has been created, then the 1988 Housing Act gives the tenant several rights over and above any agreed to by the landlord. In particular, the tenant is given 'security of tenure'. This means that at the end of the tenancy the tenant does not have to move out of the property; he has a legally enforceable right to stay on in possession. The landlord can require the tenant to leave only if he can establish a valid reason as to why he wishes to obtain possession. The only valid reasons for requiring possession are those set out in the Act. They are known as 'grounds for possession' (see pages 24–33) and include situations where the tenant has not been paying the rent regularly or the landlord wishes to occupy the house himself.

Some of the grounds for possession are known as 'mandatory grounds'. With these, on proof of the ground, the landlord has an absolute right to possession. Others, however, are 'discretionary grounds'. In the case of these grounds the landlord will be entitled to possession only if, in addition to the ground, he can also establish that it is reasonable for him to insist on possession.

Merely having a ground for possession is not sufficient,

however, whether the ground is mandatory or discretionary. The landlord still has to apply for a court order, following the correct procedure, before he can actually obtain possession (see Chapter 10).

Definition of an assured tenancy

A tenancy under which a dwellinghouse is let as a 'separate dwelling' will be an assured tenancy if and so long as *all* of the following requirements are met:

- the tenant or each of joint tenants is an individual
- the tenant or at least one of the joint tenants occupies the dwellinghouse as his only or principal home
- the tenancy is not specifically excluded by other provisions of the Act.

Each of these requirements is further examined below.

'Tenancy'
The letting must be a 'tenancy'; licences are excluded from the definition. If the occupier does not have the sole right to possession of the house then he will be a licensee, and not a tenant. (See page 67 for more details on the distinction between a tenancy and a licence.)

'House'
There is no precise definition of 'house', but in this context it is wider than the everyday use of the word. Any building designed or adapted for living in is capable of being a house, and includes lettings of whole houses as well as self-contained flats, converted barns, windmills, etc.

'Let as a separate dwelling'
The property which is let, as well as being a 'house', must be let as a 'dwelling'. If a building that would otherwise qualify as a house is let for business purposes (e.g. as an office), the tenant cannot claim that it is let on an assured tenancy merely because he decides to move in and live there. (A tenant of business

premises is likely to have other statutory protection, but this is outside the scope of this book.)

Furthermore, to qualify as an assured tenancy, the letting must be of a single dwelling only. If the property comprises two or more residential units, each intended for separate occupation (e.g. the letting of the whole of a house which has been converted into several flats), that tenancy cannot be an assured tenancy. The subletting of each of the individual flats, however, could be within the definition.

The term 'separate dwelling' is important, as it is intended to exclude the letting of accommodation which lacks some essential feature of a dwelling, such as a kitchen. So the letting of a single room without kitchen and bathroom facilities could not be an assured tenancy even if the tenant 'lived' in the room. However, if the tenant is given the right to share essential facilities with others, the letting could be an assured tenancy. The tenant must also have the right to the exclusive occupation of at least one room – otherwise it cannot be a tenancy at all. If a group of people have shared occupancy of the whole of a house, but no one has the right to exclusive possession of any one part of the house, the arrangement can only be a licence, not an assured tenancy.

Note that if the facilities are shared with the landlord, the tenancy will be excluded from the definition of an assured tenancy for different reasons (see page 22).

'If and so long as'

The status of the letting as an assured tenancy is not to be determined once and for all at the commencement of the letting; its status can fluctuate according to circumstances. For example, one requirement of the definition is that the tenant must occupy the house as his only or principal home. If this situation changes at any point during his occupation, the tenancy will no longer be assured and the tenant will lose his security of tenure.

The tenant must be an 'individual'

'Individual' in this context means a person or a group of people. Lettings to companies are therefore excluded from the definition, even though an employee or director of a company may be in occupation of the house. Lettings to limited companies are often used by landlords as a way of avoiding the grant of an assured tenancy with its security of tenure implications. However, any subletting by the company tenant could qualify as an assured tenancy, and so this should be expressly prohibited in any lettings to a company where there is a wish to avoid granting security of tenure.

The tenant's 'only or principal home'

A person's 'home' is the place in which he intends to live permanently, rather than occupy for a temporary period. The law recognises, however, that it is possible for a person to have more than one home. If this is the case, the circumstances will decide which is the tenant's principal home. It should also be noted that although the provision requires 'occupation', it need not be continuous occupation. A temporary absence, due to holidays, hospitalisation, etc., will not prevent a tenancy from remaining an assured tenancy.

Tenancies specifically excluded from the definition

Some lettings that satisfy the basic definition but fall into one of the following categories of an assured tenancy are not protected:

Tenancies entered into before the 1988 Act

Only lettings entered into on or after 15 January 1989, when the Housing Act 1988 came into force, can be assured tenancies. Any tenancy already in existence on that day remains subject to the provisions of the Rent Act 1977 (see Chapter 4).

High-value properties

Any tenancy of a house with a rateable value in excess of £750 (£1,500 in Greater London) granted before 1 April 1990 cannot be assured.

If the rent payable for a tenancy granted on or after 1 April 1990 is £25,000 or more per annum it cannot be an assured tenancy.

Tenancies at a low rent
This exclusion has also been affected by the abolition of domestic rates. Lettings made before 1 April 1990 cannot be assured if the annual rent is less than two-thirds of the rateable value of the property. For tenancies granted on or after 1 April 1990, the exclusion applies to tenancies in which the rent does not exceed £250 per annum (£1,000 per annum in Greater London).

Business tenancies
A tenancy in which the premises are occupied wholly or partly for the purposes of a business, cannot be an assured tenancy, even if the premises are the tenant's only or principal home. The traditional corner-shop with living accommodation over it is a typical example. Although it cannot be assured, such a letting may well have some protection under the statutory protections given to business tenancies.

Licensed premises
Premises licensed for the sale of alcohol for consumption *on* the premises, such as a public house, are excluded from the definition of an assured tenancy, even if the tenant lives on the premises.

Tenancies of agricultural land
Tenancies of agricultural land will be excluded even though the tenant lives on the property. (Such tenants will probably have other statutory rights under the legislation relating to agricultural holdings, but this is outside the scope of this book.)

Lettings to students
Lettings to students by specified educational bodies, e.g. most universities and colleges, are outside the definition of an assured tenancy. Note that this exception does not apply to lettings to students by landlords other than the specified universities and colleges; lettings by private landlords are capable of being assured tenancies, subject to the normal requirements being fulfilled.

Holiday lettings
A letting for the purpose of a holiday cannot be an assured tenancy. Some landlords have tried to exploit this exception by purportedly granting holiday lettings in non-holiday areas and for excessively long periods of time. However, the courts are liable to see through such schemes and will regard the letting as a fully protected assured tenancy.

Lettings by resident landlords
If the landlord lives in another part of the same building as that occupied by the tenant, it is likely that the letting will not be an assured tenancy. (For more details see page 22.)

Crown, local authority and some types of housing association lettings
Although these are excluded from the definition of an assured tenancy, lettings by local authorities and housing associations may have other protections (see Chapters 6 and 7 respectively).

Existing Rent Act tenants

The 1988 Housing Act gives assured tenants less protection in some respects (particularly with regard to rent) than that given to tenants protected by the 1977 Rent Act. Anti-avoidance provisions were therefore written into the 1988 Act so that unscrupulous landlords could not deprive their existing tenants of their Rent Act protection. Therefore, any tenancy, even if granted on or after 15 January 1989, will remain a Rent Act-protected tenancy. This will be the case even if the house let under the new tenancy is not the same as that let to the tenant under the original tenancy; a landlord cannot deprive his existing Rent Act tenants of their protection simply by granting them a letting of a different house.

The only exception to this provision is if the tenant was a protected shorthold tenant under the Rent Act 1977. Protected shortholds were the forerunners of today's assured shortholds and like them gave no security of tenure. Any new letting to a protected shorthold tenant will be an assured shorthold whether or not it complies with the normal shorthold requirements.

(For further details on assured shortholds, see Chapter 3; for protected shortholds, see Chapter 4.)

Rent control

There is no restriction on the amount of rent which can initially be charged on the grant of an assured tenancy. This is so even if there is an existing registration of a fair rent for the purposes of the Rent Act 1977 (see Chapter 4). The amount of rent to be charged is fixed by agreement between landlord and tenant. Market forces will thus prevail. However, if the landlord subsequently wishes to increase the rent, he may not be able to do so unless he follows the correct procedure.

Contractual increases

Under the normal principles of contract law, a landlord cannot change the amount of rent payable without the consent of the tenant, *unless* the terms of the tenancy allow him to do so. From a landlord's point of view, therefore, it is sensible for a term to be inserted in any tenancy agreement allowing the landlord to increase the rent, should he wish to do so.

Many informally granted tenancies contain no such provisions and landlords may find that in the case of a long-term tenancy the value of rent received is rapidly eroded by the effects of inflation, with no chance of increasing the rent or getting the tenant out of the property, owing to the security of tenure rules.

To relieve this potential unfairness, the 1988 Housing Act contains provisions enabling a landlord to increase the rent even though this is not permitted by the terms of the agreement. These provisions, however, apply only to periodic (i.e. weekly or monthly) tenancies and the procedure is somewhat complex. It is therefore still advisable to include a provision for rent increase, even in a periodic tenancy.

Statutory increases for assured periodic tenancies

If there is no provision in the tenancy agreement allowing the landlord to increase the rent, he can do so by following the procedure laid down by the 1988 Housing Act. This is a complex procedure requiring the landlord to serve a notice (in the prescribed form) on the tenant suggesting a figure for the new rent. The tenant can refer this notice to his local rent assessment committee (an independent public body) for arbitration if agreement on the new rent cannot be reached. The rent assessment committee is directed to determine the rent at which the premises might reasonably be let in the open market. There is no suggestion, however, that the rent assessment will be less than the open market rent for the house. This is not a return to the old 'fair rent' system under the 1977 Rent Act (see Chapter 4). If there is an express term in the tenancy agreement permitting rent increases, there will be no need to rely on the statutory procedure.

Increases for fixed-term assured tenancies (including shortholds)

There are no statutory provisions providing for an increase in fixed-term tenancies, e.g. one for 18 months; they apply only to periodic tenancies. In the absence of any express provision in the tenancy agreement the landlord will be unable to increase the rent during the fixed term without the agreement of the tenant.

However, once the fixed term has ended the tenant will continue in possession as a statutory periodic tenant (see above). The same provisions apply, enabling the landlord to increase the rent, even if there is no express provision in the lease.

Transferring the tenancy and subletting

A tenancy 'belongs' to the tenant and he can freely 'assign' it, i.e. sell it or give it away, to whomever he likes. Alternatively, he can sublet, i.e. grant a lease shorter than his own, or take in lodgers. This is all well and good from the point of view of the tenant but is unlikely to be acceptable to a landlord; there is little point in a landlord carefully checking the references of a tenant only to find that the tenant can then assign the tenancy to a person about whom he knows nothing. It is sensible, therefore, for the tenancy agreement to contain an express prohibition on assignment.

However, if there is no such express prohibition, the 1988 Housing Act may be of some assistance to the landlord. The Act applies only to periodic assured tenancies (including statutory periodic tenancies); like the provisions allowing increases of rent, it does not apply to fixed-term periodic tenancies (including shortholds). Therefore, in the absence of an express contractual prohibition, a fixed-term tenant will be able to assign or sublet as he chooses.

Periodic assured tenancies contain the assumption (in legal language, 'implied term') that the tenant shall not without the consent of the landlord:

- assign the whole or part of the tenancy; or
- sublet or part with possession of all or part of the property.

These prohibitions do *not* apply if a premium was paid on the grant or renewal of the tenancy. 'Premium' means payments in addition to rent (e.g. a lump sum on the grant of the lease) and also includes returnable deposits exceeding one-sixth of the annual rent.

Note that this statutorily implied prohibition does *not* prevent the taking in of lodgers or the sharing of accommodation with someone else.

Death of a tenant

A tenancy does not end with the death of a tenant. It will be passed on in the same way as the deceased's other property. On the death of a joint tenant, the tenancy will become the sole property of the survivor(s). On the death of a sole tenant the tenancy will pass to the person nominated in his will. If the tenant dies without leaving a valid will ('intestate') the decision as to whom his property will pass (this could be a spouse) will be decided according to legal rules.

The 1988 Housing Act, however, contains specific provisions dealing with the succession to a periodic tenancy on the death of a sole tenant which will override these normal rules. On the death of a sole periodic tenant the tenancy will pass to the tenant's spouse, notwithstanding the terms of the deceased's will, in all cases where the spouse has been occupying the dwellinghouse as his or her only or principal home immediately prior to the death.

'Spouse' means any person who was living with the tenant as his or her wife or husband even if they were not actually married. It does not, however, include persons of the same sex even though they may have been cohabiting; nor will succession rights apply if the deceased tenant was himself a 'successor', i.e. he gained the tenancy through any of the following means:

- as the qualifying spouse of a deceased tenant
- under the will or intestacy of a former tenant
- as the sole survivor of joint tenants
- if he succeeded to the tenancy under the provisions of the Rent Act 1977 (see Chapter 4).

Therefore only one statutory succession is possible. If there is no statutory succession because there is no qualifying 'spouse', or there has already been a succession, or the tenancy is for a fixed term, the tenancy will then pass under the will or intestacy of the deceased in the normal way. It should be noted, however, that on the death of a periodic tenant in such a situation the landlord would be able to make use of one of the mandatory grounds in order to obtain possession (see Ground 7, page 29).

The position of subtenants

The law recognises that a tenant can grant a lease giving the right to exclusive possession of the property to someone else. In this way, a subtenancy is formed. The only restriction is that this sublease must be for a shorter duration than that which remains unexpired under the landlord's own lease. So a tenant with two years left to run of his lease could grant a sublease for any period not exceeding one year and 364 days.

As between any landlord and tenant, it is irrelevant whether the landlord owns the freehold interest in the property or is himself merely a tenant. If the conditions for the creation of an assured tenancy are satisfied, then the subtenant, as against his own landlord, will have an assured tenancy with the usual protections. This will be the case even if the lease under which the landlord owns the property (the 'head-lease') prohibits subletting.

The problem, however, is that the subtenant may not always have protection against the head-landlord (i.e. the original tenant's landlord). This means that although the subtenant's own landlord may not be able to evict him, the head-landlord may be able to obtain possession against him.

The determining factor is whether or not the head-lease prohibits the granting of subleases. If it does, either expressly or by implication, then the sub-tenant will have no protection against the head-landlord once the head-lease has expired. At that point the head-landlord has an immediate right to possession without the need for any reasons or grounds for possession. Although he cannot evict the subtenant without obtaining a court order, this will be available as a matter of right.

On the other hand, if the subtenancy was *not* prohibited by the terms of the head-lease, the subtenant will have the protection of an assured tenancy against both his own landlord and any head-landlord, irrespective of whether the head-lease comes to an end or not.

This is a potential problem for landlords granting assured shorthold tenancies (see Chapter 3). Although an assured shorthold tenant has no security of tenure, any subtenancy that he grants is capable of being an assured tenancy, complete with full security of tenure which can be binding upon the head-landlord. The head-landlord is entitled to possession against the assured shorthold head-tenant but not against the subtenant – hardly satisfactory from the head-landlord's point of view. Shortholds have to be granted for a fixed term, so the restriction on subletting mentioned on page 19 will not be implied into the shorthold tenancy. A landlord granting a shorthold can avoid this problem by ensuring that the tenancy agreement contains an *express* provision prohibiting subletting. With such a provision, any subletting would not be binding upon the head-landlord.

Although a well-prepared landlord can avoid finding himself bound by the rights of a subtenant, a prospective tenant may experience difficulties in establishing that the person showing him round the property really does have the right to grant the tenancy. There is no practical way of resolving the problem. Although it is possible to find out from the Land Registry who owns a particular property, this takes time and money, and ownership of many properties is still recorded in by title deeds which are not accessible to the public.

Resident landlords

Most lettings by resident landlords are excluded from the definition of an assured tenancy, and therefore have no security of tenure. They may also have only limited protection under the protection from eviction legislation (see Chapter 9). This situation is often referred to as the 'resident landlord exception'.

The letting will be excluded from the definition of an assured tenancy if *all* of the following conditions are met:

- the dwellinghouse let forms only part of a building
- the building is not a purpose-built block of flats
- the tenancy was granted by an individual (i.e. *not* a limited company) who at the time of the grant occupied another part of the same building as his only or principal home
- the landlord has been resident at all times since the tenancy was granted.

If a landlord lives in a large house and lets part of it, or converts a house into several flats, lives in one and lets the others, the lettings will be without security of tenure. However, if the building was constructed as flats (as opposed to being *converted* into flats) the lettings will be capable of being assured tenancies even if the landlord lives in one of the flats himself.

The reason for the resident landlord exception is that it is thought unwise to give security of tenure to tenants when they are living in close proximity to the landlord. Close proximity is not considered a problem in a purpose-built block of flats – hence the exception to the normal rule.

It is not sufficient for the landlord to have been in residence just at the start of the tenancy; he must be in occupation *throughout* the tenancy for the exemption to apply. If the landlord is two or more individuals, only one of those people need be in residence at any one time. It should also be noted that temporary absences due to holiday, hospitalisation, change of ownership, or the death of the landlord, will not result in the landlord losing his exemption from security of tenure rules.

Furthermore, if the landlord moves in *after* the start of the tenancy, then the exception will not apply, even if he is still in residence when possession is being sought. If a tenant already has an assured tenancy and the landlord then moves in and grants him a further tenancy, this second tenancy will *not* be subject to the resident landlord exception even though the landlord was in residence at the start of the tenancy and remains so throughout the letting. This is an anti-avoidance provision designed to ensure that a landlord does not deprive existing tenants of their rights as assured tenants.

Security of tenure

An assured tenancy can only be brought to an end by the landlord if he obtains a court order for possession. In the case of a periodic assured tenancy, a notice to quit is of no effect. At the end of a fixed-term assured tenancy (including a shorthold), other than by an order of the court or by surrender, the tenant is entitled to remain in possession as a statutory periodic tenant. 'Surrender' consists of an agreement between landlord and tenant that the tenancy should come to an end and that the tenant will leave the property. Note, though, that the tenant can in no way be forced by his landlord to enter into this kind of agreement and that any agreement to terminate contained in the tenancy agreement will be ineffective.

Obtaining a court order for possession

The landlord can only obtain a court order for possession if he follows the correct procedure and can establish one or more of the grounds for possession set out in Schedule 2 to the Housing Act 1988. Some grounds are mandatory, i.e. the court must order possession if the ground is established, whilst others are discretionary, i.e. the court, on proof of the ground, may order possession only if it considers it reasonable to do so. The procedure for obtaining possession is set out in detail in Chapter 10. In summary, it requires the landlord to serve a notice on the tenant (a Section 8 notice), in the prescribed form. The Section 8 notice must specify the ground(s) upon which the landlord intends to rely and must give two weeks' (or sometimes two months') notice of the landlord's intention to commence possession proceedings.

The proceedings must then be commenced no earlier than the date specified and no later than 12 months from the date of service of the notice. It is possible for the court to do away with the requirement for a Section 8 notice (unless Ground 8 is being relied upon), but only if it considers it 'just and equitable' to do so.

Grounds for possession

There are two kinds, mandatory and discretionary. Grounds 1–8 below are mandatory, 9–16 discretionary.

Mandatory grounds
On proof of one of these grounds the landlord will automatically be entitled to an order for possession (assuming that he has followed the correct procedure). Most of these mandatory grounds require the landlord to have served a notice on the tenant at the start of the tenancy warning that the ground might be used against him.

The full wording of the various grounds is set out in Appendix I.

Ground 1: owner–occupier
Although often referred to as the 'owner–occupier' ground, this ground really consists of two separate situations entitling the landlord to possession.

The first part of the ground merely requires the landlord to prove that at 'some time' before the tenancy was granted he occupied the house as his only or principal home. This need not have been immediately prior to the letting; it could have been several years before. Once he has established this, he is entitled to an order for possession; he does not have to give or prove any reason why he might want possession.

The second part of the ground requires the landlord to show that the house is needed as his (or his spouse's) only or principal home. The particular circumstances of each case will be considered. The obvious danger is that an unscrupulous person might buy a house subject to a tenancy, perhaps at a very low price because of this, and then use the ground to obtain possession from the tenant. This is prevented by a proviso that the ground will not be available to a landlord who has bought a house subject to a sitting tenancy. The ground will be available, however, to a landlord who inherits the house from a deceased landlord, or who obtains it by way of a gift.

For both parts of this ground it is necessary for the landlord to have given written notice to the tenant no later than the beginning of the tenancy that possession might be recovered under this ground. Such a notice would be valid if contained in the tenancy agreement itself and need not be in any particular form; it is sufficient that it simply makes clear to a tenant that Ground 1 will be available against him.

If the notice was *not* served, then the court may use its discretion to disregard this, but only if it thinks that it is 'just and equitable' to do so. An example of this might be if there had been an oral agreement between the landlord and tenant.

This is one of the grounds which requires two months' notice of impending proceedings.

Ground 2: mortgagee exercising power of sale
It is likely that an 'owner–occupier' granting a tenancy under Ground 1 will have a mortgage on the property. If a borrower does not keep up with the payments under a mortgage, the lender's basic remedy will be to obtain possession of the house and then sell it to recover the money owed. This could pose a problem to a lender if the property is occupied by an assured tenant with security of tenure.

The power to grant leases is normally excluded by the terms of the mortgage deed unless the consent of the lender (e.g. a building society) has been obtained. Any tenancy granted by the borrower/landlord without the consent of the lender will *not* be binding upon the lender and will be in breach of the terms of the mortgage deed. Accordingly, although the landlord would not be able to obtain possession without proving assured tenancy grounds, the lender will have an absolute right to possession without the need to prove any ground. A court order would be necessary, however, to enforce this right.

A building society or other lender will usually give consent to the letting of a mortgaged property provided it is able to obtain possession against the tenant if it needs to sell the property to recover the loan. This ground is specifically designed for lenders who may wish to do this, but its availability is usually dependent upon the landlord having served a Ground 1 notice on the tenant. Sometimes, the lender will also require the borrower/landlord to give a separate notice to the tenant stating that Ground 2 will be available against him.

As with Ground 1, two months' notice of proceedings must be served.

Ground 3: out-of-season holiday accommodation

This ground is designed for the 'professional' landlord who lets out property for holiday purposes during part of the year only – holiday cottages or flats, for instance. It may be difficult to find holidaymakers to take the property during the winter months and, in order to produce some income, the landlord may wish to make the accommodation available for ordinary residential lettings. With such lettings, however, the danger is that owing to the security of tenure legislation, the landlord will not be able to obtain vacant possession when the property is once more required for holidaymakers.

This ground will be available for 'winter lets' provided that:

(1) Written notice that this ground would be available against him was served on the tenant no later than at the beginning of the tenancy. The notice can thus be included in the tenancy agreement. Note that unlike Grounds 1 and 2 this notice may not be dispensed with by the court. If the notice is not given in writing, this ground will not be available even if there was an oral discussion of the need to vacate before the beginning of the holiday period.

(2) The property has been occupied for holiday purposes at some time during the 12 months prior to the granting of the tenancy. It is therefore not available to landlords who have not previously let the house for holiday purposes.

(3) The letting is for a fixed term not exceeding eight months in length. This ground will not be available for any other type of letting, e.g. periodic tenancies, even if the correct notice was given.

Ground 4: out-of-term student accommodation

Many educational institutions let their halls of residence, flats, etc., to non-students during student vacations (e.g. for conferences). This ground enables them to ensure that they will be certain of recovering possession at the end of the letting, provided that the following requirements of the ground are complied with:

(1) Written notice that this ground would be available against him was served on the tenant no later than the beginning of the tenancy. The notice can therefore be included in the tenancy agreement. Note that unlike Grounds 1 and 2 this notice may not be dispensed with by the court, even if there had been an oral agreement between tenant and landlord.

(2) The property was let by an educational institution to students at some time during the 12 months prior to the commencement of the tenancy.

(3) The letting is for a fixed term not exceeding 12 months in length. This ground will not be available for any other type of letting, e.g. periodic tenancies, even if the correct notice was given.

Ground 5: minister of religion's house

Many religious denominations own houses for the purposes of occupation by one of their ministers. This ground enables them to let this accommodation to other tenants yet be sure of recovering possession should it be required in the future for occupation by a minister.

The following conditions must be complied with:

(1) The house must be held for the purpose of occupation by a minister of religion as a residence from which to perform the duties of his office.

(2) Written notice that this ground would be available against him was served on the tenant not later than the beginning of the tenancy. The notice can therefore be included in the tenancy agreement. Note that unlike Grounds 1 and 2 this notice may not be dispensed with by the court, even if there had been an oral agreement between landlord and tenant.

(3) The court is satisfied that the dwellinghouse is required for occupation by a minister of religion as a residence from which to carry out his duties.

Two months' notice of proceedings is required for this ground.

Ground 6: demolition or reconstruction

This ground can be used if the landlord intends to demolish or reconstruct the property or a large part of it, or to carry out substantial works. Unlike the previous mandatory grounds, there is no requirement for any warning notice to have been served prior to the granting of the tenancy.

The ground makes it clear that if the works can be carried out 'around the tenant' without possession being obtained, then the ground will not apply unless the tenant refuses to agree to the necessary arrangements.

In addition, detailed rules have been built into this ground to prevent unscrupulous landlords from using the ground when circumstances do not really justify it. As with Ground 1, it will not be available to a landlord who has bought the house since the date of the granting of the tenancy. Similarly, a landlord cannot circumvent this restriction by purchasing the property subject to a tenancy and then granting a new tenancy to the same tenant (or one of joint tenants).

Also excluded from the operation of this ground are former 1977 Rent Act tenancies which were converted to assured tenancies on a succession taking place following the death of the original tenant. For further details, see page 62.

Two months' notice of proceedings must be served by the landlord for this ground to be applicable. If the ground is established, then the landlord must pay reasonable removal costs for the tenant.

Ground 7: death

This ground is available when possession proceedings are begun within 12 months of the death of a periodic assured tenant. If the landlord is not immediately notified of the tenant's death, the 12-month time limit will run from the date on which, in the opinion of the court, the landlord became aware of the tenant's death.

Although the ground states that possession proceedings must be commenced within 12 months of the death of the tenant, landlords need to be aware that the Section 8 notice still needs to be served and to have expired before the proceedings are commenced. So, in effect, the landlord has less than 10 months from the date of death in which to serve the notice if proceedings are to be commenced within the 12-month time limit.

When an assured tenant dies, the deceased's spouse will, in certain circumstances, be entitled to succeed to the tenancy (see pages 19–20). This ground for possession will *not* be available if such a succession takes place.

Ground 8: substantial rent arrears

Under the terms of the 1977 Rent Act, rent arrears formed a discretionary ground only and the court would often exercise its discretion and refuse to order possession. For assured tenancies, however, in very limited circumstances, this ground gives a mandatory right to possession.

Firstly the arrears must be quite substantial: 13 weeks if rent is payable weekly, three months if payable monthly. In addition, the rent must be in arrears both at the date of the service of the Section 8 notice *and* at the date of the hearing. A partial payment of, say, one week of arrears just before the hearing, leaving 12 weeks of arrears, would prevent proof of the ground.

However, there are also discretionary grounds for possession based on rent arrears (see Grounds 10 and 11 below). Because of the danger of relying solely on Ground 8, it is usual for a landlord to serve a Section 8 notice and commence proceedings based on these two discretionary grounds as well as Ground 8.

Discretionary grounds

Proof of the following grounds for possession will not inevitably result in a possession order being made against a tenant. The court may only make such an order if it considers it 'reasonable to do so'. The circumstances of each individual case need to be considered; the conduct of the parties during the tenancy and any hardship likely to be suffered by either landlord or tenant will often be deciding factors.

Ground 9: alternative accommodation

A ground for possession is available if the landlord can prove to the court that 'suitable' alternative accommodation will be available to the tenant when the possession order takes effect. The accommodation does not necessarily have to be provided by the landlord.

The Housing Act 1988 sets out the circumstances to be taken into account when deciding suitability. If the landlord can obtain a certificate from the local housing authority saying that it will provide alternative accommodation for the tenant, then this certificate is deemed to be conclusive evidence that the accommodation will be 'suitable' for the needs of the tenant. In practice, however, because of the many demands on the limited accommodation available, it is most unlikely that such a certificate would be forthcoming. It may well be that, if a possession order *was* obtained, the housing authority would be obliged to rehouse the tenant because of its responsibilities to house the homeless, but that is not to say that the authority will facilitate the making of the possession order by issuing such a certificate.

Alternatively, the landlord will have to show that the proposed alternative accommodation is 'reasonably suitable' for the needs of the tenant and his family as far as location, furnishings, size and rent are concerned. Furthermore, the accommodation must be available for letting on an assured tenancy, not an assured shorthold, nor one to which mandatory Grounds 1 to 5 might apply.

The landlord must serve two months' notice of proceedings to use this ground.

As with mandatory Ground 6, the landlord must pay

reasonable removal expenses for the tenant if possession is ordered.

Ground 10: *rent arrears*

This is the first of the two discretionary grounds based on rent arrears and is available if the landlord can prove that:

- some rent lawfully due from the tenant is unpaid on the date when possession proceedings are started
- some rent was in arrears at the date of the service of the notice relating to the proceedings.

Unlike mandatory Ground 8, which requires at least 13 weeks' rent to be in arrears both at the date of the service of the Section 8 notice and at the date of the hearing, no minimum amount of rent needs to be outstanding for this ground to be established, nor need the amount outstanding be the *same* at the date of the start of proceedings as at the date of the Section 8 notice. Indeed, as long as *some* rent was in arrears at the date of the Section 8 notice and at the start of the possession proceedings, it does not matter whether there is any rent in arrears at all when the hearing date arrives.

It is sensible, therefore, for a landlord to use this ground in addition to Ground 8 to cover the possibility of a tenant paying off some or all of the arrears prior to the hearing date. It is vital to remember, though, that this is only a discretionary ground; the court can only make an order for possession if it considers it reasonable to do so. If all the arrears have been discharged by the date of the hearing, it may not consider it reasonable to order possession.

Ground 11: *persistent delay in paying rent*

For this ground, there is no need for any rent to be in arrears at all, either at the date of service of the Section 8 notice, or when the possession proceedings are commenced, or at the date of the hearing. All that needs to be established is that the tenant has 'persistently delayed paying rent'.

Ground 12: *breach of covenant*

This ground will be available if the tenant has broken any express or implied obligations placed on him under the tenancy.

The ground would be available if, for example, the tenant had broken the *implied* obligations not to sublet or if he had broken an *express* obligation to keep the house properly decorated. The ground will still be established even if the breach has been remedied by the date of the hearing, although the court may not consider it reasonable to order possession if this is the case.

Ground 13: waste or neglect
This ground is available if the condition of the house, or of any common parts, has deteriorated due to the acts or neglect of the tenant or anyone living with him. Fair wear and tear will obviously be excluded from this ground. Often there will be an express item in the tenancy agreement to the same effect, in which case Ground 12 would be available as well.

If the deterioration is caused by someone other than the tenant, the ground can only be established if the tenant has failed to take such steps as 'he ought reasonably to have taken for the removal of the lodger or subtenant'. Presumably, the extent of the deterioration would be a relevant factor in deciding what amounts to 'reasonable steps'.

Ground 14: nuisance
This ground consists of two separate instances which will give the landlord a right to claim possession.

The first instance is if the behaviour of the tenant or any other person residing in the house has caused nuisance or annoyance to adjoining occupiers. Persistent playing of loud music late at night might be sufficient to establish this part of the ground.

The second part of the ground will be established if the tenant or any other person living in the house has been convicted of using or allowing the house to be used for an illegal or immoral purpose. Note that *using* the house for illegal or immoral purposes is not sufficient; there has to have been a conviction. However, if these acts have caused nuisance or annoyance, then the first part of this ground could be used.

Like Ground 13, Ground 14 can apply even if the tenant has not breached the terms of the tenancy. If he has, Ground 12 will be available as well. However, unlike Ground 13, the tenant will be in breach whether or not he has taken reasonable steps to remove the offender.

Ground 15: damage to furniture etc.

This ground is available if the condition of any furniture provided by the landlord under the terms of the tenancy has deteriorated owing to the acts or neglect of the tenant or any other person living in the house. Fair wear and tear will obviously be excluded from this ground. As with Ground 13, in the case of damage caused by a lodger or subtenant, the ground will only be established if the tenant has failed to take reasonable steps to remove the offender.

If there is an express term in the tenancy prohibiting damage etc., then Ground 12 will also be available.

Ground 16: former employee

This ground will be available if the house was originally let to the tenant because he was employed by the landlord, and that employment has now come to an end. It does not matter who brings the employment to an end; nor is it necessary for the landlord to prove that he requires the accommodation to house a new employee. This, however, may well be a relevant factor when the court decides whether or not it is reasonable to order possession.

Note, finally, that not all employees housed by their employers will have tenancies. If it is essential for the employee to occupy the house in order for him to carry out the terms of his employment, then he will be a 'service occupant' – a mere licensee, and therefore the arrangement could not amount to an assured tenancy. The landlord would then have an absolute right to possession on termination of the employment.

Q *I have an assured monthly tenancy. My landlord tells me that he will be increasing the rent next week. I can't afford the extra but he says that I've got to pay. I don't want to lose my flat. What is my position?*

A Unless the tenancy agreement allows him to (it should be checked), a landlord can change the amount of the rent originally agreed only if he follows the procedure laid down by the 1988 Housing Act. This requires the landlord to serve a notice on you in the form laid down by the Act. If he does not follow the correct procedure, you do not have to pay the increase.

If you refuse to pay, there is no risk of your losing your flat. Rent arrears are a ground for possession (see Grounds 8, 10 and 11) only if the rent is 'lawfully due' from you. As the landlord was never entitled to increase the rent, it will not be lawfully due and so cannot be used as the basis of possession proceedings.

Once you have stated your legal rights, simply refusing to pay and virtually challenging the landlord to take you to court is not likely to create good relations between you. It would be better to try to have a friendly chat with your landlord and explain that he is not adopting the right procedure. Ask how long it is since the rent was last increased and whether there might be some compromise. If it was several years ago, it may well be possible, and fair, to agree a modest increase in line with inflation. An amicable settlement, rather than a confrontation based on your strict legal rights, may be more beneficial to you in the longer term.

Q *I have an assured monthly tenancy and have recently become pregnant. My landlord says that he doesn't allow children and that I must leave my flat before the baby is born. I have nowhere else to go. Can he make me leave?*

A In the short term, no, but it all depends upon the terms of the agreement you signed. Many tenancy agreements do prohibit children (and animals), but such a provision will not be implied in a tenancy (see page 75). So unless children are expressly prohibited by your tenancy agreement, the landlord has no legal grounds on which to object to your baby. In the absence of any ground for possession against you, you are fully protected in your continued occupation of the flat.

If children *are* prohibited by the terms of your agreement, the landlord may well try to obtain possession against you. However, as you have security of tenure as an assured tenant he must follow the correct procedure (see Chapter 10). Breach of a term of the tenancy agreement is a discretionary ground for possession (Ground 12), which means that even though you have broken the term of the lease, the court will order you to leave only if it considers it reasonable to do so. The hardship that you and your baby would suffer would certainly be taken into account by the judge when considering whether or not to make a possession order.

Q *I am the landlord of a small terraced house which is let on an assured monthly tenancy. Owing to financial problems I am selling the flat in which I live and would like to obtain possession of the property I let. Is this possible? (The tenant has always been a good tenant and pays his rent on time.)*

A In order to obtain possession you will need to go to court, following the correct procedure (see Chapter 10), and you will then need to prove a ground for possession. The second part of Ground 1 (a mandatory ground) allows a landlord to obtain possession where the house is required as his only or principal home. However, Ground 1 will be available only if notice was given to the tenant no later than the beginning of the tenancy that this ground might be cited. If, as is likely, the notice was not given, the ground will only be available if the court thinks it just and equitable to make an exemption. It is important to remember that courts will also look at the situation from the tenant's point of view and you would probably have difficulty in obtaining an order for possession.

Q *I inherited a small house from my grandmother last year. It was let on a weekly tenancy to friends of hers. I have just discovered that the tenants moved out a few months ago and that the house is now occupied by their nephew. I was happy for my grandmother's friends to live in the house but the nephew is not paying the rent regularly and is holding noisy all-night parties which are disturbing the neighbours. Can I obtain possession?*

A In order to obtain possession you will need to go to court, following the correct procedure (see Chapter 10), and prove one of the grounds for possession laid down by the Act. One of the grounds (Ground 12) is that the tenant has broken one of the terms of the tenancy agreement. Assuming that there is nothing to the contrary in the tenancy agreement and that no premium (payment in addition to rent) was charged at the start of the tenancy, it is an implied term of the agreement that the tenants may not transfer the tenancy without the landlord's consent, so this ground may well be available to you. If the noisy parties have been causing annoyance to the neighbours, you might be able to establish Ground 14 as well. The snag, however, is that both of these grounds are discretionary, i.e. the court does not have to order possession, even on proof of the ground; it will make an order for possession only if it considers it reasonable to do so, which will depend upon the view it takes of the circumstances. The fact that you have been accepting rent from the nephew for some time may well be taken into account in deciding whether it is reasonable to make an order under Ground 12.

Q *When my grandmother was ill I moved into her house in order to look after her. I had to give up my own flat to do this. I lived with her for nearly two years but she died last month. The landlord now says that I must leave the house. Do I have to go?*

A The tenancy did not end on your grandmother's death. In the absence of a surviving spouse who would be entitled to succeed to the tenancy under the terms of the 1988 Housing Act, the tenancy would pass under her will or according to the rules of intestacy. Therefore, it may well not have passed to you. Even if it has, the landlord has a mandatory right to possession under Ground 7. However, he must follow the correct procedure and commence proceedings within 12 months of learning of your grandmother's death. Your only hope is that the landlord does not commence proceedings within this 12-month time limit, for then any claim under Ground 7 will not be successful.

CHAPTER 3

ASSURED SHORTHOLD TENANCIES

ASSURED shorthold tenancies were introduced under the 1988 Housing Act on 15 January 1989. They were designed to breathe new life into a moribund letting market which had suffered 30 years of dramatic decline. The amount of accommodation available for letting to private tenants had shrunk rapidly as landlords feared that they would not be able to recover possession of their property. The particular set of advantages offered by the assured shorthold tenancy has proved immensely popular with landlords and in consequence the letting market has been boosted enormously. None the less, this type of tenancy contains specific requirements of which one needs to be aware.

An assured shorthold tenancy is a fixed-term tenancy of at least six months' duration, with no security of tenure. This means that once the fixed term has run out the landlord has an absolute right to recover possession, provided that he follows the correct procedure. Prior to the granting of the tenancy, however, the landlord must give a notice to the tenant, in the prescribed form (see page 41), warning him of the effect of entering into an assured shorthold. This notice cannot be dispensed with and it is vitally important for the landlord to follow this procedure.

Shortholds are popular with landlords precisely because they ensure that the premises can be recovered on a given date. The only disadvantage from a landlord's point of view (apart from the need to comply with the pre-condition mentioned above) is that the tenant is given the right to refer the rent initially payable to a rent assessment committee for its consideration. However, the committee may reduce the rent only if it is 'significantly higher' than the rents of other comparable properties; there is therefore no danger of the rent being reduced to a level below the open market rent for the property.

Definition of an assured shorthold tenancy

Experience shows that many lettings purporting to be shortholds do not in fact comply with all the requirements of the legislation. A letting which does *not* comply with all these requirements will almost certainly amount to an ordinary assured tenancy, giving the tenant full security of tenure and the landlord a very different set of problems.

An assured shorthold tenancy is an assured tenancy which:

- is granted for a fixed term of not less than six months
- contains no power for the landlord to terminate it during the first six months
- was preceded by giving the prescribed shorthold notice to the tenant.

These requirements are examined below.

Assured tenancy

An assured shorthold tenancy is merely a type of assured tenancy. It must therefore comply with all the requirements of an assured tenancy and none of the specific exclusions must apply (see pages 12–16).

A shorthold cannot be granted to an existing tenant by the same landlord under an ordinary assured tenancy (or to one of joint tenants). This is so even if the lettings are not of the same premises. The effect of this is to prevent landlords from depriving their existing assured tenants of security of tenure by purportedly granting them a shorthold. Similarly, as with all assured tenancies, a shorthold cannot be granted to an existing Rent Act-protected or statutory tenant.

Minimum six-month fixed term

The initial grant of a shorthold cannot be for a periodic tenancy, i.e. a weekly or monthly tenancy. It must be for a fixed term and for a minimum duration of six months. There is, however, no maximum length, despite the connotations of the term 'shorthold'. It is legally possible to have a shorthold granted for, say, 21 years or more; there are, however, practical reasons connected with rent control (see pages 45–6) why long shortholds would not be a good idea from a landlord's point of view.

Many shortholds are granted for the minimum six-month period. In such a case care must be taken to ensure that the tenant is given a right to occupy for the full amount of the minimum period. The six-month period will run from the date when the tenancy is signed; it cannot be backdated.

Problems are likely to arise where a tenancy agreement is drawn up containing a fixed termination date and there is then a delay in the agreement being signed, so that by the time it has been signed less than six months until the fixed termination date remain. Such a letting would amount to an ordinary assured tenancy, giving the tenant full security of tenure. For instance, a tenancy granted 'from and including 1 January 1994 until 30 June 1994' but not actually signed until 15 January 1994 could not be an assured shorthold tenancy.

Care must also be taken when letting for the minimum six-month term when the agreement states that the term runs 'from' a specified date. Under the normal legal rules that govern the interpretation of documents, that date is then excluded from the term. So a letting 'from 1 January 1994 until 30 June 1994' will exclude 1 January from the term and will therefore be for one day less than the minimum six months required. Again, this would amount to an ordinary assured tenancy. The correct wording to use to grant a minimum six-month tenancy should be 'from *and including* 1 January 1994 . . .'.

No power for landlord to terminate during first six months

Even if a minimum period of six months is granted, any power, however expressed, which would or might allow the landlord to terminate the tenancy within the first six months of the tenancy will prevent the tenancy from amounting to a shorthold. Clauses permitting termination outside that period are not prohibited, but if they are within the initial six months an ordinary assured tenancy will be created, giving the tenant full security of tenure. These 'break clauses' can be useful to a landlord who wishes to grant, say, a five-year fixed-term tenancy, but wants to be able to recover possession before then, should the need arise (e.g. if he needs vacant possession to sell the house or to occupy it himself).

A clause allowing the tenant to terminate the tenancy during the first six months would be quite valid. Such a provision, however, will not be implied. A tenant entering into a shorthold is, therefore, legally bound to pay the rent and perform the other obligations under the tenancy agreement for the full term entered into – even if he chooses to leave before the end of the fixed term. This must be borne in mind by all prospective tenants before entering into long fixed-term tenancies of any sort; if there is a chance that they might have to move on before the stated termination date, they should try to get the landlord to agree (in writing) to their being able to leave early, should they wish to do so, or to grant a shorter tenancy.

Prescribed shorthold notice for prospective tenants

As the tenant under an assured shorthold will have no security of tenure, he has to be given a notice prior to the grant of the tenancy warning him of this fact. This notice must be in writing and in the prescribed form, i.e., it must conform precisely to the layout and content required by the law. An oral 'notice' is in no way sufficient. Note, however, that the content of the necessary form has changed twice since the introduction of assured shortholds on 15 January 1989 and care must be taken to ensure that the shorthold notice served is the correct one as at the date of service. The current version of the form is set out on pages 41–3. A landlord wishing to grant a shorthold must ensure that the notice he gives to the tenant contains identical wording to this and that the layout is kept to as closely as possible. It is possible to obtain printed copies of the form from any law stationer.

The previous versions of the form are very slightly different. Neither the form in use prior to 17 August 1990 nor the form valid from 17 August 1990 until 31 March 1993 include the *final* sentence of point 3 which reads: 'If the rent includes a payment for council tax, the rent determined by the committee will be inclusive of council tax.' In addition, the form valid before 17 August 1990 includes a *fourth* point which reads: 'This notice was served upon you on . . . [date inserted]'.

Housing Act 1988 section 20

Notice of an Assured Shorthold Tenancy

- Please write clearly in black ink.

- If there is any thing you do not understand you should get advice from a solicitor or Citizens Advice Bureau, before you agree to the tenancy.

- The landlord must give this notice to the tenant before an assured shorthold tenancy is granted. It does not commit the tenant to take the tenancy.

- This document is important, keep it in a safe place.

To:

Name of proposed tenant. If a joint tenancy is being offered enter the names of the joint tenants.

1. You are proposing to take a tenancy of the dwelling known as:

from | / | /19 | to | / | /19 | *The tenancy must be for a term certain of at least six months.*

day month year   day month year

2. This notice is to tell you that your tenancy is to be an assured shorthold tenancy. Provided you keep to the terms of the tenancy, you are entitled to remain in the dwelling for at least the first six months of the fixed period agreed at the start of the tenancy. At the end of this period, depending on the terms of the tenancy, the landlord may have the right to repossession if he wants.

3. The rent for this tenancy is the rent we have agreed. However, you have the right to apply to a rent assessment committee for a determination of the rent which the committee considers might reasonably be obtained under the tenancy. If the committee considers (i) that there is a sufficient number of similar properties in the locality let on assured tenancies and that (ii) the rent we have agreed is significantly higher than the rent which might reasonably be obtained having regard to the level of rents for other assured tenancies in the locality, it will determine a rent for the tenancy. That rent will be the legal maximum you can be required to pay from the date the committee directs. If the rent includes a payment for council tax, the rent determined by the committee will be inclusive of council tax.

To be signed by the landlord or his agent (someone acting for him). If there are joint landlords each must sign, unless one signs on behalf of the rest with their agreement.

Signed

Name(s) of landlord(s)

Address of landlord(s)

Tel:

If signed by agent, name and address of agent

Tel:

Date: 19

Special note for existing tenants

- Generally if you already have a protected or statutory tenancy and you give it up to take a new tenancy in the same or other accommodation owned by the same landlord, that tenancy cannot be an assured tenancy. It can still be a protected tenancy.
- But if you currently occupy a dwelling which was let to you as a protected shorthold tenant, special rules apply.
- If you have an assured tenancy which is not a shorthold under the Housing Act 1988, you cannot be offered an assured shorthold tenancy of the same or other accommodation by the same landlord.

Both landlords and tenants under existing shortholds should check that the *correct* version of the form was used as at the date that the notice was given. The importance of using the correct version *cannot be emphasised too strongly*: if it is not, the letting will not amount to a shorthold and the landlord will not be entitled to possession unless he can establish ordinary assured tenancy grounds (see Chapter 2).

The notice must be given to the tenant before the tenancy agreement is entered into; it cannot be included in the tenancy agreement itself. It is best to ensure that there is an adequate interval between the service of the notice and the signing of the tenancy agreement to give the tenant the opportunity of digesting the contents of the notice. In the case of joint tenants, all of the prospective tenants should be given the notice.

A prospective landlord should bear in mind that he will have to prove that he gave this notice to the tenant in order to be entitled to a possession order from the court. It is therefore advisable for a landlord to give two copies of the notice to each prospective tenant and have them each sign and return one copy to acknowledge receipt before signing the tenancy agreement.

The copy to serve as acknowledgement of receipt should bear a notice at the bottom, typed or handwritten, along the following lines:

I acknowledge that a notice in the same terms as set out above was given to me on ... [insert date when notice was given to tenant]

Signed ....

Dated .... (date of signature)

This acknowledgement must be returned to the landlord before the tenancy agreement is signed and the tenant allowed to take possession of the property.

The court has no power to dispense with these notice requirements, even though it might be just and equitable to do so. The regulations do allow service of a form 'substantially to the same effect' as the prescribed form, but this is not a provision to be relied upon except in an emergency.

Rent control

On the granting of the tenancy, the landlord may charge whatever rent he likes – although this will probably be governed to some extent by market forces, so if he tries to charge too much he may not find anyone interested in taking the letting. It is worth noting, however, that there is no statutory restriction on the amount of rent chargeable. Any existing registration of a 'fair rent' under the provisions of the Rent Act 1977 (see Chapter 4) can be ignored.

The rent assessment committee

An assured shorthold tenant may, at any time, apply to the local rent assessment committee for the determination of the rent which, in the committee's opinion, the landlord might reasonably be expected to obtain under the shorthold tenancy. Notice of this right is in the shorthold notice given to the tenant prior to the tenancy. However, the committee cannot make such a determination unless there is a sufficient number of similar dwellinghouses in the locality let on assured tenancies to suggest a norm *and* the rent payable under the shorthold is significantly higher than the rents charged for these.

There is, therefore, no question of the rent being assessed at a level lower than the market rent for the premises; this is not a return to the 'fair rent' system used under the Rent Act 1977, which frequently resulted in a rent of less than the market value being fixed. Therefore a landlord is at risk of a lower rent being fixed only if he is charging significantly more than the market rent for the house.

If a rent is determined by the committee it will become the maximum rent chargeable for the property throughout the remainder of the fixed term. This is despite anything to the contrary in the tenancy agreement – and there is no provision for this figure to be increased during the fixed term, no matter how long that might be. It is for this reason that landlords are best advised to avoid the grant of long shortholds. In the case, for example, of a 21-year shorthold, a rent fixed in the first year would continue to apply for the remainder of the term, despite any provisions in the agreement allowing the landlord to increase the amount of the rent.

However, this is a once-and-for-all right given to the tenant. Once the rent has been determined by the committee, no further application for the fixing of a different figure can be made by either landlord or tenant, even if market rents change in the meantime.

The rent determined by the committee applies only during the particular tenancy in question. It will not limit the amount of rent chargeable under any subsequent letting of the same property, even if this is between the same landlord and tenant. At the end of the fixed term, and assuming that no new tenancy is granted, a statutory periodic tenancy will arise. The landlord may increase the rent payable under this tenancy to above that assessed by the committee, by following the procedure laid down for increasing rents under ordinary assured tenancies (see pages 17–18). Twelve months must have passed since the assessment before this procedure can be followed.

It is not possible for the tenant to refer the rent to the rent assessment committee once the original term of the shorthold has expired. This is so even if a new letting is entered into between the same parties and irrespective of whether an application was made during the original shorthold. Note also that only one application to the committee can be made. Once the rent has been determined by the committee, it cannot be resubmitted for a further determination, even if the original determination was many years before.

Expiry of a shorthold

At the end of the fixed term, the tenant is allowed to remain in possession as a statutory periodic tenant, but the tenant still has no security of tenure. The court must still make an order for possession if the landlord has followed the correct procedure. The tenant must be given not less than two months' notice of the landlord requiring possession. For details see Chapter 10.

Granting a new tenancy

If the parties are the same, a new tenancy of the same (or substantially the same) property will be deemed to be a shorthold unless the landlord serves notice on the tenant that the new letting is not to be a shorthold.

The effect of this 'deeming' provision is that any new tenancy will be a shorthold even though it does not comply with the normal shorthold requirements. So no shorthold notice need be served and the letting need not be for a fixed term, i.e. a periodic shorthold is permissible, and any fixed term need not be for a minimum period of six months.

A further feature of these deemed shortholds is that the tenant has no right to refer the rent to the rent assessment committee. This is the case whether or not an application was made to the committee during the initial shorthold term. If a rent was determined by the committee during the initial term this will not limit the amount of rent chargeable by the landlord under the new tenancy agreement.

Obtaining possession

The court must order possession, on or after the ending of a shorthold and provided that the landlord has followed the correct procedure. This requires the landlord to serve a notice on the tenant (the Section 21 notice) giving him at least two months' notice that he requires possession. Full details of this procedure are set out in Chapter 10.

Other grounds for possession

A shorthold is a type of assured tenancy and so during the fixed term the mandatory and discretionary grounds which apply to ordinary assured tenancies can also apply. For full details of these see pages 24–33. This means, for instance, that mandatory Ground 8 and discretionary Grounds 10 and 11 (all of which relate to rent arrears) can be used during the term of the shorthold should the landlord be faced with a defaulting tenant. However, as with other assured tenancies, these grounds can be used during the fixed term only if the tenancy agreement contains provisions allowing this.

Q *I have a 12-month shorthold tenancy with six months left to run but I need to move to a different town because of my job. Can I leave if I give the landlord a month's notice?*

A Legally speaking, you can leave at any time, but you will still be obliged to continue paying the rent until the end of the 12 months. You agreed to pay the rent for the full 12 months and unless there is something written into the tenancy agreement allowing you to leave early, the rent is still due from you. Your only hope is to approach the landlord on an informal basis and explain your problem. He may be sympathetic and agree to let you off future payments of rent, particularly if you find someone to take over the flat when you leave.

Q *I have a 12-month shorthold with six months left to run. Last week the landlord told me that he was putting up the rent next week. Can he do so?*

A Only if there is something in the tenancy agreement which gives him the right to do so. If there is not, the rent must remain fixed until the end of the fixed term. He can then increase the rent, but if you do not accept that the proposed increase is reasonable, you can insist that he follows the procedure laid down for assured tenancies (see pages 17–18) and the matter can then be referred to a rent assessment committee for an independent assessment of the correct amount of rent payable. An amicable settlement is obviously preferable.

Q *Before I took my tenancy, my landlord told me that it was going to be a shorthold, but no written notice was ever given to me. The tenancy has now come to an end and the landlord says I must move out next week. Do I have to go?*

A You do not have to give up possession unless and until the court orders you to do so. In the case of a shorthold tenancy, a landlord is entitled to a possession order as of right. However, your tenancy cannot be a shorthold as the correct shorthold notice was not given to you prior to the letting. The notice must be in writing – an oral notice is not sufficient. Your tenancy is, therefore, an ordinary assured tenancy and in order to obtain a possession order the landlord will need to follow the correct procedure and establish one of the assured tenancy grounds (see Chapter 2).

Q *I granted a six-month shorthold tenancy which expired three months ago. Since then I have continued to accept rent from the tenant on a monthly basis, but there has been no further agreement between us. I now want the tenant to leave, but she says she does not have to do so as she now has an ordinary assured tenancy with full security of tenure. Is she right?*

A No. On the ending of a shorthold and in the absence of the grant of a new tenancy, the tenant remains in occupation as a statutory periodic tenant. But this implied tenancy is still a shorthold, unless the landlord informs the tenant that it is not to be a shorthold. Even if a new tenancy had been expressly granted, that too would be a shorthold unless the landlord tells the tenant otherwise. So you have an absolute entitlement to possession, provided you follow the correct procedure (see Chapter 10).

CHAPTER **4**

THE RENT ACT 1977

ANY TENANCY originally entered into prior to 15 January 1989 is likely still to be governed by the provisions of the Rent Act 1977. The Housing Act 1988 changed the law for tenancies created on or after 15 January 1989, but basically did not alter the position with regard to tenancies already in existence on that date.

There are, therefore, still many thousands of Rent Act tenancies in existence today, although their numbers are likely to decline as the years go by and tenants leave.

Furthermore, it is still possible for new Rent Act tenancies to be created even today, albeit in very limited circumstances (see page 16).

Rent Act tenants are given wide-ranging security of tenure, similar in many ways to that given to tenants under assured tenancies. This means that, as in assured tenancies, a landlord will be able to obtain possession of the property only if he goes to court and establishes one of the approved grounds for possession.

The main difference between Rent Act tenancies and assured tenancies is that the former are subject to rent control, the 'fair rent' system which tends to keep rents below those which would prevail in the open market.

On the death of a Rent Act tenant, succession rights also tend to be more generous than those applying to assured tenancies. Sometimes, however, the new tenant will not inherit Rent Act protection: he will become an assured tenant under the Housing Act 1988 (see pages 62–3).

Protection under the Rent Act is given to 'protected tenancies' and 'statutory tenancies', as described below.

Protected tenancies

A protected tenancy exists where a dwellinghouse was 'let as a separate dwelling' (see page 12, where the similarly worded requirement for an assured tenancy under the Housing Act 1988 is discussed).

Note, however, that in contrast to the Housing Act's requirement for an assured tenancy there is no need under the Rent Act for the letting to be to an individual, nor does the house need to be the tenant's only or principal home. Therefore a letting to a limited company can be a protected tenancy.

There are various exceptions which are generally very similar to those for assured tenancies, e.g. lettings by resident landlords, holiday lettings, tenancies at a low rent (see pages 14–16). Lettings where the rent includes payment for board or service are also excluded from the definition of a protected tenancy; this includes lettings where meals are provided or the landlord cleans the rooms. There is no similar exclusion for assured tenancies.

Protected tenancies can be either periodic or for a fixed term; tenants have rent control and succession rights, but not necessarily security of tenure. To have security of tenure, a Rent Act tenant must qualify as a 'statutory tenant' on the ending of the protected tenancy.

Statutory tenancies

A statutory tenancy is the device by which security of tenure is given. At the end of the protected tenancy, the tenant will become a statutory tenant only 'if and so long as he occupies the dwellinghouse as his residence'. The tenant will continue to have the benefit of rent control and will also have security of tenure, i.e., he may be evicted only if the landlord goes to court and establishes one of the grounds for possession laid down by the Rent Act.

There is no requirement that the dwellinghouse should be occupied as the tenant's only or main residence; for Rent Act purposes it is accepted that a person may have two homes and that there may be a statutory tenancy of either or both of them. Note also that a company tenant can be a protected tenant but not a statutory tenant; as with assured tenancies, the tenant must be an individual (see pages 13–14).

As a statutory tenancy can arise only on the ending of a protected tenancy, it means that in order to obtain possession against a protected tenant a landlord must first of all terminate the protected tenancy, e.g. by serving notice to quit. If the tenant does not qualify as a statutory tenant, the landlord will immediately be entitled to a court order for possession. If a statutory tenancy does arise, the landlord will have to establish one (or more) of the grounds for possession laid down below. As with assured tenancies, some of these are mandatory and so the court must order possession on proof of the ground, but many are discretionary and the court can only order possession if it considers it reasonable to do so. Many of the assured tenancy grounds for possession were based on Rent Act grounds and reference should be made to the equivalent assured tenancy ground where relevant (see Chapter 2). The Rent Act 1977 grounds are called 'Cases' and are set out in the 15th Schedule to the Act.

Discretionary grounds for possession

Case 1
'Where any rent lawfully due from the tenant has not been paid, or any obligation of the protected or statutory tenancy . . . has been broken or not performed.'

This case should be compared with Grounds 8, 10, 11 and 12 for assured tenancies. Note, in particular, that non-payment of rent is only a discretionary ground, no matter how great the amount of the arrears. If you are a landlord seeking possession from a Rent Act tenant owing to rent arrears, note that even if you establish that the arrears exist you may still not obtain a possession order because the court may well not consider it reasonable to make such an order.

Case 2

'Where the tenant or any person residing or lodging with him or any subtenant of his has been guilty of conduct which is a nuisance or annoyance to adjoining occupiers, or has been convicted of using the dwellinghouse or allowing the dwellinghouse to be used for immoral or illegal purposes.'

This case is identical, in effect, with assured tenancy Ground 14.

Case 3

'Where the condition of the dwellinghouse has, in the opinion of the court, deteriorated owing to acts of waste by, or the neglect or default of, the tenant or any person residing or lodging with him or any subtenant of his and . . . where the court is satisfied that the tenant has not, before the making of the order in question, taken such steps as he ought reasonably to have taken for the removal of the lodger or subtenant, as the case may be.'

This is virtually the same as assured tenancy Ground 13 and shares its problems. Unlike Ground 13, however, it does not extend to damage etc. caused to the common parts of the building.

Case 4

'Where the condition of any furniture provided for use under the tenancy has, in the opinion of the court, deteriorated owing to ill-treatment by the tenant or any person residing or lodging with him or any subtenant of his, and . . . where the court is satisfied that the tenant has not, before the making of the order in question, taken such steps as he ought reasonably to have taken for the removal of the lodger or subtenant, as the case may be.'

See also assured tenancy Ground 15.

Case 5

'Where the tenant has given notice to quit and, in consequence of that notice, the landlord has contracted to sell or let the dwellinghouse or has taken any other steps as the result of which he would, in the opinion of the court, be seriously prejudiced if he could not obtain possession.'

This ground has no equivalent under assured tenancies. It is necessary for Rent Act tenancies, as a statutory tenancy (with security of tenure) is formed on the ending of the protected tenancy, no matter how it may have ended. So if a tenant gives notice to quit, a statutory tenancy will still arise and the landlord will not be entitled to possession unless he can prove one of the grounds laid down by the Act. This could place him in difficulty if, thinking that the tenant is about to vacate the property, he enters into a contract to sell with vacant possession. Without this case, the landlord would have no right to possession if the tenant subsequently changed his mind and decided not to vacate after all.

There is no need for an equivalent ground for assured tenancies, as the Housing Act 1988 makes it clear that if an assured tenancy comes to an end by virtue of a tenant's notice to quit, then there is no security of tenure for the tenant and the landlord will have an absolute right to possession without further proof.

Case 6

'Where, without the consent of the landlord, the tenant has . . . assigned or sublet the whole of the dwellinghouse. . . .'

This case will apply whether or not there is any express prohibition on assignment or subletting (i.e. transferring the tenancy) in the tenancy agreement. It is applicable only to protected tenancies; a statutory tenant who assigns or sublets is no longer protected by the Rent Act. It has no direct equivalent in assured tenancies, but it is an implied term of every periodic assured tenancy that the tenant will not assign without consent (see page 19). A breach of this implied term would then render the tenant liable to a possession order against him under Ground 12 (see page 31).

Case 7

This has now been repealed and is therefore no longer applicable.

Case 8

'Where the dwellinghouse is reasonably required by the landlord for occupation as a residence for some person engaged in his whole-time employment, or in the whole-time employment of some tenant from whom or with whom, conditional on housing being provided, a contract for such employment has been entered into, and the tenant was in the employment of the landlord or a former landlord, and the dwellinghouse was let to him in consequence of that employment and he has ceased to be in that employment.'

This is similar to assured tenancy Ground 16. For this case to apply, the landlord needs to establish that the property was let to the tenant because he was employed by the landlord. Unlike assured tenancy Ground 16, however, the landlord also has to prove that he reasonably requires the house for accommodation for another employee. Whether he 'reasonably' requires possession will be dependent upon the facts of the case.

Case 9

'Where the dwellinghouse is reasonably required by the landlord for occupation as a residence for: (a) himself; (b) any son or daughter of his over 18 years of age; (c) his father or mother; or (d) . . . the father or mother of his wife or husband, and the landlord did not become landlord by purchasing the dwellinghouse or any interest therein. . . .'

It should be noted that a court may not order possession under this case if, having looked at all the circumstances, it is satisfied that greater hardship would be caused by granting the order than by refusing it. Obviously, the question of hardship will depend upon the facts of the particular case, but factors such as the availability of alternative accommodation to the respective parties and their respective financial circumstances will be relevant.

This case will be available to a landlord whether or not he has resided in the property prior to the letting and there is no need for any warning notice to have been served on the tenant prior to the letting (*cf* Case 11 and assured tenancy Ground 1). Remember also that, unlike those grounds, this is only a discretionary ground for possession. Even if the landlord proves the ground and overcomes the 'greater hardship' test, the court will still order possession only if it considers it reasonable to do so.

Case 10
This case allows possession to be claimed if the tenant has sublet part of the house at a rent greater than is legally permitted. The principle ties in with the fair rent system (see page 60), which fixes the maximum rent that can lawfully be charged on a Rent Act letting, and is little used.

Suitable alternative accommodation
Although not allocated a case number, the Rent Act 1977 also allows the court to order possession on this ground, but again only if it considers it reasonable to do so. See assured tenancy Ground 9 for a discussion of what amounts to 'suitable' alternative accommodation.

Mandatory grounds for possession

If the landlord can establish one of these mandatory grounds, then the court has no discretion and must order possession, notwithstanding whether it is reasonable to do so or whether any hardship will be caused to the tenant.

Case 11
Where a person who occupied the dwellinghouse as his residence (in this case referred to as 'the owner-occupier') let it . . . and (a) not later than [the date of the commencement of the tenancy] the landlord gave notice in writing to the tenant that possession might be recovered under this case; and (b) the dwellinghouse has not . . . been let by the owner-occupier on a protected tenancy with respect to which the condition mentioned in paragraph (a) above was not satisfied; and (c) the court is of the opinion that . . . *one* of the following conditions has been satisfied:

(1) The dwellinghouse is required as a residence for the owner

or any member of his family who resided with the owner when he last occupied the dwellinghouse as a residence.

(2) The owner has died and the dwellinghouse is required as a residence for a member of his family who was residing with him at the time of his death.

(3) The owner has died and the dwellinghouse is required by a successor in title as his residence or for the purpose of disposing of it with vacant possession.

(4) The dwellinghouse is subject to a mortgage made by deed and granted before the tenancy, and the mortgagee is entitled to exercise a power of sale and requires possession of the dwellinghouse for the purpose of disposing of it with vacant possession.

(5) The dwellinghouse is not reasonably suited to the needs of the owner, having regard to his place of work, and he requires it for the purpose of disposing of it with vacant possession so that he can use the proceeds to purchase another house which would be more suited to his needs.

This case must be distinguished from the superficially similar Case 9. Unlike Case 9, it is dependent upon the service of a warning notice prior to the letting and the landlord must have resided in the house at some time prior to the letting. However, if the court decides that it is just and equitable to make an order for possession, it has the power to dispense with the notice requirement. The basic ground is that the landlord requires possession from the tenant so that the house can be used as a residence for himself or a member of his family. Note, however, that in the case of a family member, he or she must have lived in the house with the landlord the last time he resided in the property, otherwise the ground will not be established.

Case 12
This allows possession to be claimed by a landlord who has purchased a house as a prospective retirement home, but lets it in the meantime. There is no need for prior residence (*cf* Case 11), but the availability of the case is again dependent upon a warning notice having been given no later than the commencement of the tenancy. This notice requirement can, however, be

dispensed with in the same circumstances as in Case 11. The landlord will then be entitled to possession on retirement or in the circumstances set out in points 2 and 3 of Case 11.

Case 13

This is virtually identical to assured tenancy Ground 3 about lettings of holiday accommodation out of season and requires the giving of a warning notice prior to the letting. As with that ground, the prior warning notice cannot be dispensed with.

Case 14

This case is relevant to lettings of student accommodation by specified educational institutions. It is almost identical to assured tenancy Ground 4 and is again dependent upon the giving of a warning notice prior to the letting.

Case 15

This case involves the letting of houses kept for occupation by ministers of religion and is identical to assured tenancy Ground 5.

Cases 16, 17 and *18* relate to lettings of farmhouses and houses to people employed in agriculture when the house is required for occupation by a new employee.

Case 19

This case gives the landlord of a protected shorthold tenancy (see page 63) a mandatory right to possession. As it is unlikely that any protected shorthold tenancies are in existence, this case is no longer of practical significance.

Case 20

This case allows members of the armed forces who acquired and let houses during their years of service to obtain possession in similar circumstances to owner-occupiers under Case 11. Although a warning notice needs to have been served on the tenant no later than the commencement of the tenancy, there is no need for the landlord to have occupied the house prior to the letting. The requirement for this warning notice may be dispensed with in the same circumstances as under Case 11.

The fair rent system

With both protected and statutory tenancies, the amount of rent the landlord may charge for the property is subject to control. The Rent Act 1977 set up a register of 'fair rents' for dwelling-houses: once a rent has been registered for a property, that figure becomes the maximum amount chargeable under any present or future protected or statutory tenancy of the property.

The rent is assessed by the rent officer – a local authority official – in accordance with criteria laid down by the Act. Under normal market forces, the scarcity of accommodation available to let tends to push up rents beyond the means of many people, but the rent officer works on the assumption that there is no shortage of accommodation (even though there might be), and the rent assessed is often considerably lower than it would otherwise be. The existence of the fair rent system is obviously a valuable asset for Rent Act tenants, but is often viewed less favourably by landlords, who consider that it prevents them from receiving an adequate return on their investment.

Applying for a fair rent

Assuming that no fair rent is registered in respect of the property, on the grant of a tenancy the landlord can charge whatever rent the market will bear. However, at any time during the period of the tenancy, the tenant may apply for a fair rent assessment. The landlord cannot in any way prevent an application being made. Once assessed, the rent then becomes the maximum payable, *despite* the existence of any higher agreed figure in the tenancy agreement. Furthermore, the fair rent may not then be exceeded in any new letting of the house, whether to the same or to a different tenant. The only way in which the landlord can increase the rent is by applying on his own behalf to the rent officer for the assessment of a higher fair rent. However, he cannot make such an application within two years of an earlier fair rent assessment unless there has been a material change in the condition of the dwelling or the terms of the tenancy.

On the fixing of a fair rent, therefore, a tenant is assured of a minimum period of two years before an increase in rent can take place. There are, however, exceptional circumstances where it is possible for a landlord to apply for a new rent within the two-year period, such as if the landlord has carried out improvements to the property which mean the rent is no longer a fair rent. Without this exception to the rule, landlords would have to wait an inordinately long time before receiving an increased rent to reflect the amount of money spent on the property. However, there is no exception to the two-year rule in cases where the landlord pays the council tax. If the amount payable increases during the two-year period, this does not entitle the landlord to apply for a higher rent; he will have to wait until the end of the two years before he can apply.

Mechanism for increasing a registered fair rent

Once a fair rent has been registered, the only way in which the landlord can increase the rent is by obtaining the registration of a higher fair rent. However, even if the landlord succeeds in this – note the phasing provisions mentioned above – he cannot immediately claim the first part of the increase. He must first of all give the tenant a 'notice of increase'; this must be in the form laid down by Parliament. When it is given, payment of the increased amount of rent can be backdated, but not for more than four weeks and not to a date prior to the registration of the new amount.

Over-payment of rent

If a tenant has been over-charged by a landlord, he can claim back the excess amount he has paid. However, only the over-payments from the last two years can be recovered. Any rent over and above the amount permitted by the Rent Act is deemed to be 'irrecoverable', meaning that the landlord cannot sue for it or commence possession proceedings based on non-payment.

Succession to Rent Act tenancies

On the death of a statutory or a protected tenant, that person's spouse will automatically become the statutory tenant of the house, provided that he or she was living in the house at the time of death. In the case of unmarried cohabitees, the legislation states that a 'person living with the tenant as husband or wife' will become the statutory tenant. However, no succession is possible for cohabitees of the same sex, whatever the circumstances.

In the case of deaths occurring prior to 15 January 1989, any member of the deceased's family who had lived with him at the time of death and for at least six months prior to death would have become a statutory tenant. In the case of deaths taking place on or after 15 January 1989, for a family member to succeed he or she needs to have been living with the deceased for at least two years prior to death.

However, when such deaths occur the family member will become entitled only to an assured tenancy, not a statutory tenancy. The main effect of this is that, although the tenant will still have wide-ranging security of tenure, he will lose the benefit of the fair rent system. This means that the rent could well be liable to a substantial increase to bring it up to the levels of open-market rents chargeable under assured tenancies. As with other assured periodic tenancies, if the tenant does not accept the landlord's suggested increase, he has the right to refer the rent to a rent assessment committee for an assessment of what the market rent ought to be (see page 17).

In the case of deaths prior to 15 January 1989, two successions were permitted. On the death of the first successor, the same succession rules would apply in favour of that person's spouse or family member. However, in the case of the death of a first successor after 15 January 1989, a second transmission is only possible in very limited circumstances. An individual is entitled to a second succession only if he was *both* a member of the original tenant's family *and* a member of the first successor's family, *and* had resided with the first successor for at least two years prior to the first successor's death. Note that there is no requirement for the second successor to have lived with the original tenant at all; it is sufficient for him to be a member of the original tenant's family, although often, of course, he will have resided with the original tenant.

This complicated formula is designed to cover a situation where the original tenant was, say, a man living in the house with his wife and child. On his death, a first transmission will occur in favour of his wife; on her death, a second transmission is then possible in favour of the child, provided that the child satisfies the residence requirement. Note that this second successor will always take the tenancy as assured tenant.

Protected shorthold tenancies

Protected shorthold tenancies were introduced by the Housing Act 1980 but few remain in existence today.

The protected shorthold was the precursor of the assured shorthold and shared some of its characteristics. It had to be for a fixed period and be preceded by the giving to the tenant of a warning notice. Unlike the assured shorthold, however, it had to be for a duration of at least 12 months. At the end of the fixed term the landlord had a mandatory right to possession under Rent Act Case 19 (see page 59). However, the procedure for obtaining possession was very complex and had to be approached with care if the landlord was to be successful.

The effect of the Housing Act 1988 was to phase out these protected shorthold tenancies. It provided that any new letting on or after 15 January 1989 to a protected shorthold tenant would be an assured shorthold (whether or not the normal assured shorthold requirements were complied with). It is this provision, coupled with the short duration of most protected shortholds, that ensured its rapid demise after the implementation of the 1988 Act.

Q *I moved into my flat in 1988. The rent has always been quite reasonable, but a new landlord has now taken over and has put the rent up so much that I cannot afford to pay it. What can I do?*

A Your tenancy is governed by the Rent Act 1977. As such, you have the right to apply at any time for a 'fair rent'. This will be assessed by the rent officer according to criteria laid down by the Act. Once a fair rent has been assessed it then becomes the maximum payable for the flat. You should contact your county council rent officer as soon as possible for advice on how to apply for a fair rent.

Q *I took a weekly tenancy of a house in 1987. In 1992 I was granted a new tenancy of the same house at a higher rent. The landlord now wants me to leave the house. Do I have to go?*

A You are still a fully protected Rent Act tenant. Although the new tenancy in 1992 was created after the Housing Act 1988 came into operation, as an existing Rent Act tenant you remain protected by that Act. The landlord can only obtain possession by going to court, and only then if he can establish one of the Rent Act grounds.

CHAPTER 5

GRANTING A TENANCY OR A LICENCE: CHOICES FOR THE LANDLORD

WHILE previous chapters have looked at the different types of security of tenure that may govern a short-term letting of residential property, this one considers in more detail how to go about letting property.

From the landlord's point of view it makes good sense to try to choose an arrangement that will ensure recovery of possession when the letting ends. Permanent security of tenure may offer substantial benefits to tenants, but it can be a problem for landlords. They find that their assets are tied up in a property of which they cannot get vacant possession, without which they cannot realise their investment. The market for tenanted property is very small and then only at a much lower price than if vacant possession were available. This is a particular problem if the sale proceeds are required to finance the purchase of another house in which the landlord needs to live.

Fortunately for the landlord, because there is little private property available to let with security of tenure, his desire to let without security should not unduly depress the amount of rent he can expect to receive.

A tenant wishing to rent a property with permanent security of tenure will therefore have difficulties – unless an error is made by the landlord. Because of the risk and consequences of error, prospective landlords should approach the letting of their property with care. Letting agents are one option worth considering.

Letting agents

The use of letting agents is certainly convenient from the landlord's point of view as it takes away the problems of finding a tenant and collecting the rent. However, the quality of service provided by letting agents varies considerably, as do their charges. Finding a reputable agent is best done through personal recommendation; otherwise, it may help to visit a number of agencies as a prospective tenant. If details of the houses to let are well presented, the agent may be worth further consideration; agents who do not have full details of the properties available are best avoided.

It is safest to choose an agent who is a member of one of the various professional bodies who represent estate agents. This should guarantee some degree of competence and a right to appeal to a third party should a dispute arise. Members of the Royal Institution of Chartered Surveyors (RICS), the Incorporated Society of Valuers and Auctioneers (ISVA) and the National Association of Estate Agents (NAEA) should all provide an efficient service. Note, however, that no agent can guarantee that a tenant will pay the rent regularly.

A typical charge for finding tenants for a fixed-term tenancy will be 10 per cent of the rental for the initial letting period (plus VAT). When the rent is being collected by the agency the charge is likely to be 15 per cent of the rent. If action is required to chase up rent arrears there may be a further charge. A reputable agency will obtain and check the references of its tenants (e.g. from an employer) to help ascertain that the tenant can afford the rent.

Another option to consider is the full letting service offered by some agents. As well as finding the tenant(s) they will collect the rent and manage the property during the tenancy. This is likely to be more expensive.

Most letting agents make no charge to tenants. Agents that ask prospective tenants to pay a fee to be put on their books usually offer no guarantee that accommodation will be found, or that the money can be recovered.

The difference between a tenancy and a licence

The distinction between these two is important, because if someone has a tenancy he 'owns' the right to occupy the property in question. He can, subject to the terms of the lease, dispose of ownership or use it as he wishes. Moreover, if the landlord sells the freehold in the property, his tenancy will still be binding on any purchaser, even if he does not know of the tenant's existence.

A licence, on the other hand, gives the tenant no such benefits. He cannot transfer it to anyone else, and if the landlord disposes of his freehold, whether by sale, a gift or on death, the tenant's licence will not be binding on the new owner. Most of the security of tenure legislation which has been enacted protects only tenants. Occupiers who have a licence will find that they have only limited statutory protection (principally against eviction without a court order, see Chapter 9), but no security of tenure. So on the ending of a licence the landlord has an absolute right to possession.

The incentives to property-owners to grant licences rather than tenancies are obvious. The courts, however, are quick to detect sham arrangements and may declare an arrangement to be a tenancy, and therefore capable of having security of tenure, even if the parties have called it a licence.

Exclusive possession

An essential requirement of a tenancy is that the tenant should be given exclusive possession of the property. If the tenant does not have exclusive possession, then the arrangement cannot be a lease; it amounts only to a licence.

Exclusive possession includes the tenant's right to exclude all others, including the landlord, from the premises. It means that the tenant alone has the right to live there. There need not just be one tenant; a joint tenancy, where up to four people are jointly given the right to exclusive possession of the property, is also possible.

In certain circumstances, such as a family arrangement or an act of friendship or generosity, a licence may also confer exclusive possession. Normally, however, in a commercial arrangement where rent is being paid, the conclusive factor, based on the House of Lords decision in the leading case of Street *v* Mountford [1985], is whether or not exclusive possession is actually being given to the occupier. In deciding this, the courts will look at the substance and effect of the agreement as well as the wording. In this House of Lords case, a tenant had been given a purported licence to occupy a single-bedded flat. Despite the agreement alleging that she was to share occupation with the landlord, it was held that in reality she had exclusive possession and so the arrangement was actually a tenancy. The 'label' placed on the arrangement by the parties is therefore not conclusive.

Sharing arrangements

Commonly a group of people, often students or young people at the outset of their working lives, are given the right to share a flat or house. Whether they are licensees or tenants will often depend upon whether they came looking for accommodation together or separately. If they all came along together and signed the same agreement, they will be joint tenants. But even if the landlord had got them to sign separate agreements, they would probably still be tenants and not licensees. The case of Antoniades *v* Villiers [1988] bears this out. A young couple were looking for accommodation together. They each signed a separate agreement, described as a 'licence agreement', to share a one-bedroomed flat. Each agreement provided that the 'licensor' also had the right to occupy the premises and that he might license others to share occupation with the 'licensees'. The House of Lords held, however, that the arrangement was clearly a lease and that the young couple were joint tenants, with exclusive possession of the flat, even though they had signed separate agreements. The terms allowing occupation by the landlord or others were clearly not intended to be operative. It would be ridiculous to contemplate that the landlord intended to share the one bed in the flat with the young couple or that he intended to allow others to do so.

At the same time as the Antoniades *v* Villiers case, the House of Lords also heard the case of A.G. Securities *v* Vaughan. In this case the premises comprised a flat which had four bedrooms plus a bathroom, kitchen, etc. The flat was occupied by four people who were selected by the owner and who did not previously know one another. Each had arrived at a different time and each had paid a different amount for the use of the flat. Each was given the right to share the flat with the other three, but no one had exclusive possession of any part of the flat, not even a bedroom. The owner did not dictate which bedroom each was to occupy; this was left to be decided amongst the current occupiers. These arrangements were held to constitute genuine licences.

Using a licence to avoid security of tenure

Property-owners can only make safe use of licences to avoid the security of tenure legislation in a situation such as that of A.G. Securities, described above. The premises must be capable of being shared by a group of people, so a licence could not be used in the case of a self-contained one-person flat. Even so, great care must be taken. The licence agreement must be carefully drafted to ensure that exclusive possession is not granted for any part of the premises. If, for example, the agreement gives the exclusive right to occupy one bedroom, together with the right to share the remainder of the house, this will give rise to a tenancy of the bedroom, which would be capable of being an assured tenancy. Equally, if the occupants are friends or others seeking accommodation together, it is likely that even separate well-drafted agreements would be construed as a joint tenancy (as in the Antoniades *v* Villiers case).

To avoid such uncertainties, many property-owners may be better served by making use of assured shorthold tenancies, which give the landlord an absolute right to possession at the end of the term – provided the formalities are observed.

Granting a tenancy

A tenancy has to be created by deed unless it takes effect on the day it is granted and is for a term not exceeding three years and at the best rent which can reasonably be obtained without taking a premium. If such conditions are complied with, no formalities are required and so the tenancy could be granted orally. However, oral agreements are *not* recommended; in the case of any future disputes about the terms of the letting, a written tenancy agreement is obviously highly desirable.

Furthermore, if no deed is used and a court subsequently decides that one should have been, it could result in the tenant gaining a tenancy with full security of tenure, not necessarily what the landlord intended.

The deed itself can be a very simple document. Nowadays, a written agreement which at the end simply states 'Signed as a deed' followed by the signatures of landlord and tenant, is sufficient. It no longer has to be 'sealed' as was formerly the case. The only other requirement is that each signature should be witnessed, the witness signing underneath the signature he is witnessing. It is not necessary for the same person to witness both signatures. For further details, specimen tenancy agreements appear in Appendices II and III.

The pros and cons of assured shorthold tenancies

As previously stated, most lettings nowadays are assured shorthold tenancies. The big advantage of these is that the landlord is certain to obtain possession at the end of the letting. The disadvantage is that the rent can be referred to a rent assessment committee (see page 45), but few tenants take advantage of this right. There is also a certain lack of flexibility in that lettings must be for a fixed term (as opposed to periodic), and the fixed term must be for a minimum of six months. However, as the initial fixed-term letting can be followed by any kind or length of letting, which will still be a shorthold, this is rarely a problem. As long as the landlord is careful to give the correct notice beforehand and complies with all the requirements, the shorthold is the most sensible form of letting from his point of view.

Certain other forms of letting are also worthy of consideration, however.

Licences

As stated above, licences should *only* be used in the kind of sharing arrangement mentioned on pages 68–9. They have an advantage over shortholds in this sort of arrangement in that they are easier to set up (there is no need for a warning notice), and there are no initial restrictions on duration or, at any point, on the amount of rent payable.

Company lets

A letting to a company cannot be an assured tenancy, owing to the requirement that the tenant must occupy the house as his only or principal home (see page 14). Some landlords, therefore, let only to company tenants, and ask any prospective individual tenants to buy an off-the-shelf company in order that the property can then be let to that company. The company will then be prohibited from subletting, although a 'director', i.e. the person who has just bought the off-the-shelf company, would be allowed to live in the property rent-free. As this arrangement cannot be an assured tenancy, the landlord will have an immediate right to possession at the end of the letting. There are no restrictions on the length of the letting and no rent control.

However, academics frequently argue that this kind of company let should not be allowed by the courts as the arrangement is a sham; what it really amounts to is a letting to an individual in actual occupation. Although this argument has had little success in the courts, it is perhaps best to avoid the problem and use a shorthold instead.

Using the resident landlord exception

If a resident landlord, i.e. someone who lets part of the house in which he is living (see page 22 for details), the letting can not be an assured tenancy. So, again, there is no security, no rent control and no worries about complying with shorthold complexities. However, there are other problems. In particular, the resident landlord exception applies only if the landlord is resident throughout the tenancy; if the landlord ceases to reside, then the tenancy will become an assured tenancy with full security of tenure. Although the landlord may have no intention of giving up residence, his circumstances may change; it is sensible, therefore, not to rely exclusively on the resident landlord rule. In all cases it is safest to set up an assured shorthold tenancy. Although the letting cannot be a shorthold when the landlord is resident (as it is not an assured tenancy), if the landlord should cease to reside, the letting will then become an assured shorthold rather than just an ordinary assured tenancy.

Using a mandatory ground for possession in an ordinary assured tenancy

The grounds most likely to be applicable to the private landlord are Grounds 1 and 3 (see pages 24 and 26 respectively). These need to be considered separately.

Ground 1: owner-occupier
Potentially, this ground will be available to a large number of landlords. Many home-owners let their homes when they cannot find a buyer, and the first part of this ground seems exactly suited to such people. Remember that as long as the landlord has occupied the property as his home at some time prior to the letting and gives the appropriate warning notice, he will have a mandatory right to possession at the end of the letting. He does not have to give any reason for wanting possession, so the ground will be available whether he wants to live in the house again or to sell with vacant possession. The use of this ground has the advantage over a shorthold in that the letting need not be for a fixed term and there is no risk of the rent being challenged.

However, a shorthold will probably still be preferable in the case of a sole property-owner. This is because possession is only available under this part of the ground if the person seeking possession is the landlord who previously lived there. So, if a sole landlord dies and possession is required by his personal representatives or his beneficiary, it will not be available under this part of Ground 1. The second part of Ground 1, which gives a mandatory right to possession if the house is required as a residence, *would* be available to a new landlord – provided that he wanted to live there. The ground does not allow possession if it is only required to facilitate a sale, as might well be necessary.

In the case of co-owners, the ground is a viable alternative to a shorthold, since the death of one would not prevent the survivor obtaining possession under the first part of the ground.

Ground 3: out-of-season holiday accommodation
Obviously this ground is suitable only for landlords who let a property for holiday purposes during part of the year. It enables them to let the property for residential use when a holiday let is not available and still be certain of recovering possession. Note that the requirement for a warning notice cannot be dispensed with. The fact that the letting can be for less than six months (but still for a fixed term) and that there is no possibility of a challenge to the rent makes it preferable to a shorthold. A further big advantage over a shorthold is that only two weeks' notice of intention to start proceedings is required, should it prove necessary to evict the tenant.

Letting procedure

How much rent to charge

Assuming that the landlord has decided upon the type of tenancy (or licence) he intends to grant, the next step is to decide upon the amount of rent he wants to charge. If he is putting the property in the hands of letting agents, they will advise on this. Otherwise, he should look in the local newspaper and letting agents' offices and compare rents for houses similar to his own. This will then give him some idea of the market rent for his type of property in the area.

Finding a tenant

Assuming that the landlord is not using a letting agent (see page 66), an advertisement in the local press or a shop window is probably the most effective method of finding tenants. It is usually wise to avoid letting to friends (or friends of friends), as disputes over repairs and vacating the property at the end of the tenancy are more likely to occur and tend to be more difficult to resolve in such circumstances.

Taking up references

References should most certainly be taken up. Usually, two types of reference should be obtained: a personal reference as to the tenant's good character and a financial reference from a bank or employer as to his ability to pay the rent. Sight of the last couple of months' pay slips or a letter from an employer verifying annual salary should be sufficient as a financial reference. Unlikely though it is that the referee could in any way be held responsible if things do not work out during the tenancy, a tenant who is unable to provide any sort of reference is best avoided.

Taking a deposit

It is usual for the landlord to take a deposit, often the equivalent of a month's rent, as security against any damage done by the tenant or failure to pay the rent regularly. Provisions should be inserted in the tenancy agreement dealing with this (see pages 78–9).

Guarantors

If a tenant, e.g. a student, or someone who has only recently started working, is unable to provide a financial reference but is otherwise acceptable, the landlord would be well advised to ask for a guarantor. A parent or other person should sign the agreement to promise to meet the rental payments and other financial obligations should the tenant fail to do so. The guarantor's ability to pay should be checked as for a tenant.

Mortgagee's consent

It is bound to be a term of the landlord's mortgage, if he has one, that he cannot let the house without the lender's consent.

If he does let without consent, this will entitle the lender to take possession of the house and sell it in order to recover the amount owing to them. Lenders will usually consent if mandatory Ground 2 will be available to them (see page 25). They may require a Ground 2 notice to be given to the tenant.

The terms of the agreement

Many residential lettings are entered into quite informally, but this can be a recipe for disaster. A written agreement that sets out the rights and responsibilities of both parties is essential. Landlords should realise that when they let their property the law will normally allow the tenant to do more or less what he or she likes with the premises. If any particular activity is to be prohibited then this must be written into the agreement.

At the back of the book are samples of two tenancy agreements which should be suitable for the needs of most landlords: Appendix II is a sample assured shorthold tenancy agreement (see page 211) and Appendix III a sample fixed-term tenancy agreement using mandatory Ground 1 (see page 218). This is suitable for a longer-term lease as it includes a clause allowing the landlord to increase the rent during the term, should he wish to do so. It also includes a clause allowing the landlord to bring the tenancy to an end prior to the ending of the fixed term by giving the appropriate notice.

Note the following in connection with the sample agreements.

Description of the property
The property should be clearly defined, including, for example, the number or precise location of the house or flat, as appropriate.

Inventory of contents
If the house is being let furnished, a detailed inventory of all the contents should be drawn up and attached to the tenancy agreement.

Payment of rent
Express provision should be made for payment of rent in advance. Otherwise the common law implication is that rent is

payable in arrears. Payment intervals must also be stated, whether weekly, fortnightly, monthly, quarterly or yearly. If any other intervals are chosen, assured tenancy mandatory Ground 8 may not be available to the landlord (see page 29). Note that if payment at weekly intervals is chosen then the landlord must provide the tenant with a rent book.

Interest on arrears
In the case of rent arrears, the landlord will not be entitled to interest unless and until he commences proceedings. It is advisable, therefore, to include an express term in the agreement allowing the landlord to add interest to any arrears at a specified rate.

Water charges
Provision should be made as to who is responsible for the payment of water charges. The implication in the absence of express provision is that the tenant must pay them. In short-term lettings the landlord will often accept responsibility for them; if so, there should be some provision in the agreement allowing the landlord to increase the rent to take account of any increase in water charges during the tenancy.

Council tax
Council tax has been payable throughout the UK since 1 April 1993 on 'dwellings', i.e. houses or self-contained units such as flats. Liability for the tax generally falls on the person in occupation, i.e. the tenant. However, if the property is in multiple occupation, the landlord will be responsible. The definition of multiple occupation includes any dwelling inhabited by people who do not constitute a single household, i.e. where each occupier has the right to occupy part of the house only or where they are mere licensees paying no rent. Many sharing arrangements amount to multiple occupation and the landlord will pay the council tax. The rental figure charged should reflect this fact and a provision should be inserted allowing the landlord to increase the rent to take into account any increase in council tax during the tenancy. In cases other than multiple occupation, the tenancy agreement should contain

provisions stating that the rent is exclusive of council tax and requiring the tenant either to pay it to the local authority or to reimburse the landlord should he become responsible for payments.

Repairs to property

Section 11 of the Landlord and Tenant Act 1985 applies to the majority of lettings. Where the tenancy is for a term of less than seven years (see page 108), this imposes an obligation on the landlord to repair, amongst other things, the structure and exterior of the house. However, provision needs to be included allocating responsibility for non-structural internal repairs and decoration which are not covered by the landlord's implied obligation. Without such an express provision neither landlord nor tenant would be under any obligation to attend to such matters. The sample agreements impose this liability upon the tenant.

Use of property

Despite the fact that the letting is of a dwellinghouse, the law will allow the tenant to use the property for whatever purpose he chooses unless the tenancy agreement provides otherwise. It is usual, therefore, to restrict the use of the property to that of a single private dwellinghouse and also to impose obligations on the tenant not to cause nuisance or annoyance to the neighbours nor to damage the house or contents in any way.

Insurance of property

If the house is let on a short lease, the landlord will normally insure the premises, given that he has the most valuable interest in the house. However, the activities of the tenant could affect the validity of the insurance policy or the amount of premium payable by the landlord, and so terms should be included obliging the tenant not to do or omit to do anything which might have an effect on the insurance.

Assignment of the tenancy

It is essential that the landlord retains control over who is permitted to occupy his house. Under common law, a tenant can freely assign the tenancy to whomever he wishes. Although there is an implied term in most periodic assured tenancies prohibiting assignment without consent (see pages 18–19), this should not be relied upon. It is not always implied and will not be implied in fixed-term lettings, e.g. shortholds. An absolute prohibition on assignment rather than a qualified restriction is advisable; in this way the implied provision that the landlord may not withhold his consent unreasonably is avoided.

Subletting the property

As with assignment, an absolute prohibition on subletting is desirable. In the case of a shorthold, it is essential. In the absence of such a provision a shorthold tenant could grant a sublease which would be an ordinary assured tenancy and which would then be binding as such upon the head-landlord (see page 21). The prohibition on subletting implied by Section 15 of the Housing Act 1988 will not be implied into a fixed-term shorthold (see page 21).

Address for service

Under Section 48 of the Landlord and Tenant Act 1987, no rent is lawfully due from a tenant unless and until the landlord has given the tenant notice in writing of an address in England and Wales at which notices (including notices in proceedings) can be served upon him. It is sensible to include this address for service in the tenancy agreement (the samples provided do this) as this avoids the need for service of a separate notice and the possible problems of proving such service. The address given need not be the landlord's residence; it could be the address of an agent such as the landlord's solicitor.

Deposit

It is usual for a landlord to take a deposit from a tenant to provide security against non-payment of rent or damage to the property or its contents. The amount is often the equivalent of one month's rent, but could be more in the case of furnished lettings owing to the higher risk involved. The tenancy agreement should state the circumstances in which the landlord may keep back the deposit and when it would become repayable to the tenant. Provision should also be made for what would happen to the deposit on a change of landlord (i.e. it should be handed over to the new landlord), and the earning of interest. In case the landlord has to use the deposit during the term of the tenancy for any purpose, provision for the tenant to make up the deficit forthwith should be included.

Rent review

In a fixed-term tenancy it is sensible to include a provision allowing the landlord to increase the rent to take account of the effects of inflation. Without such a provision an increase in rent is not permissible without the tenant's agreement. Although rent review provision is probably not necessary for fixed-term tenancies not exceeding 12 months, i.e. the duration of most shortholds, a simple provision has been included in the second sample agreement (see page 225).

Break clauses

A break clause is a term in a lease which allows the party specified to bring the lease to an end even though it has not yet run its full length. In the case of fixed-term tenancies (including shortholds), a break clause in favour of either the landlord or the tenant may be appropriate. In the case of a shorthold it is essential to ensure that the landlord's break clause is not exercisable during the first six months of the letting, since such a clause would fall foul of the basic requirements of a shorthold (see pages 39–40) and so convert the letting into an ordinary assured tenancy. A landlord's break clause is included in the second sample tenancy agreement (see page 225). In the case of joint tenants, a provision should state whether it is necessary for *all* of the joint tenants to agree to the exercise of the break clause. If either the landlord or tenant terminates a lease in accordance with a break clause, neither party will be liable on the terms of the lease.

Children and pets

If children and pets are to be prohibited, an express provision must be included.

Mandatory grounds for possession

Where the landlord is intending to rely on one of the mandatory grounds for possession which require service of a warning notice on the tenant, e.g. in the case of an owner-occupier using Ground 1, this may be included in the agreement. The sample agreement on page 218 includes both a Ground 1 notice and also a Ground 2 notice should this be required by the landlord's mortgagee. Note, however, that it is *not* sufficient for a shorthold notice to be included in the tenancy agreement; it must be served on the tenant *before* the tenancy agreement is signed.

Forfeiture by tenant

A forfeiture clause allows a landlord to terminate a fixed-term lease prior to the expiry of the fixed term if the tenant fails to comply with his obligations under the tenancy (non-payment of rent, for example). Although it is not possible to forfeit an assured tenancy – it can only be terminated as laid down by the Housing Act 1988 – a forfeiture clause is still essential in any fixed-term assured tenancy of any length, including a shorthold. This is because the tenancy may at some future date cease to be assured, in which case the forfeiture clause could then be used. More importantly, some of the grounds for possession may, if the tenancy agreement makes the relevant provision for this, be exercisable during the fixed term. This provision can take any form, therefore the forfeiture clause should make it clear that termination can be made using Grounds 2 or 8 of the mandatory grounds and Grounds 10 to 15 of the discretionary grounds. The sample tenancy agreement on page 218 includes such a provision.

Q *I want to take in a lodger to improve my financial position. My landlord says I can't and that if I do he will throw me out. Can he do this?*

A It all depends upon the terms of your tenancy agreement. If this prohibits taking in lodgers, then you would be in breach of the terms of your letting, and this may entitle the landlord to seek possession against you. However, if the agreement is silent, you would have the right to take in a lodger.

Q *I share a house with several other students. The landlord has given us a week's notice to quit. Do we have to go?*

A Check the terms of your agreement. You are probably occupying the house under a licence. If so, you have no security of tenure and the landlord therefore has an absolute right to possession once he has terminated your right to occupy. However, assuming that you do not have a fixed-term arrangement, he must give you four weeks' notice to leave and he cannot force you to go without obtaining a court order.

CHAPTER 6

PUBLIC SECTOR TENANCIES

ALL LOCAL authority and some housing association lettings are specifically excluded from being assured tenancies under the Housing Act 1988 and from being protected tenancies under the Rent Act 1977. Such lettings have their own system of protection under the Housing Act 1985. They are known as 'secure tenancies', giving the tenant extensive security of tenure but no control over the amount of rent charged. There are also succession rights on the death of a secure tenant.

Definition of a secure tenancy

A secure tenancy is a tenancy or licence for a dwellinghouse let as a separate dwelling at any time when both the landlord condition and the tenant condition are satisfied. These terms are explained below.

'Tenancy or licence'

Unlike assured and protected tenancies, the terms of a secure tenancy expressly include a licence to occupy. However, the legal distinction between a licence and a tenancy (see page 67) is still significant, as a licence can amount to a secure tenancy only if it confers the right to exclusive possession on the occupier. As described earlier, exclusive possession can be conferred under a genuine licence only in very exceptional circumstances (see pages 67–8).

'Let as a separate dwelling'

For the significance of the term 'let as a separate dwelling', see page 12.

'At any time when'

The use of the phrase 'at any time when' shows that the status of a tenancy can change during its lifetime depending upon whether the landlord condition and the tenant condition (see below) are satisfied. If either condition ceases to apply, the tenancy will no longer be secure.

'The landlord condition'

The landlord condition dictates that the interest of the landlord should belong to one of a specified list of bodies. These include:

- a local authority (most likely)
- a New Town corporation
- an urban development corporation
- the Development Board for Rural Wales.

'The tenant condition'

The tenant condition dictates that the tenant must be an individual who occupies the dwellinghouse as his or her only or principal home. In the case of joint tenants, all of them must be individuals (see pages 13–14), but only one need occupy the property as his or her only or principal home.

Exceptions

Even though the landlord condition and the tenant condition might be satisfied there are 12 situations in which lettings will not amount to a secure tenancy. These include:

(1) Fixed-term leases exceeding 21 years. Note that a periodic tenancy, i.e. a weekly or monthly tenancy which may be or has already been in existence for 21 years or more, will *not* be excluded under this provision.

(2) Premises occupied by an employee of the landlord where his contract of employment requires him to occupy the house for the better performance of his duties. Many lettings to police officers and firefighters will also be excluded.

(3) Tenancies granted to the homeless.

(4) Dwellinghouses forming part of agricultural holdings, as defined by the Agricultural Holdings Act 1986.

(5) Premises occupied for business use.

(6) Lettings to students.

(7) Licences to occupy almshouses.

Security of tenure

A secure tenancy may not be brought to an end by the landlord unless he first obtains a court order for possession; a notice to quit is therefore of no effect. At the end of a fixed-term secure tenancy the tenant is entitled to remain in possession as a periodic tenant. Note that this rule does not prevent the *tenant* from terminating a periodic tenancy by giving notice to quit.

In order to obtain an order for possession the landlord must both follow the correct procedure and establish one (or more) of the grounds for possession laid down by the Housing Act 1985 (see pages 86–90). Unlike assured tenancies under the Housing Act 1988 and protected tenancies under the Rent Act 1977, the Housing Act 1985 does not include any mandatory grounds.

Obtaining a court order

Before the court will allow the commencement of proceedings to obtain possession the landlord must have given notice to the tenant in accordance with Section 83 of the Housing Act 1985. This prescribed notice must give particulars of the ground for possession on which the landlord intends to rely.

The landlord must set the ground out clearly so that the tenant knows precisely what is alleged against him. If the ground is *not* stated with sufficient clarity, the tenant may have cause to claim that the notice is invalid. If so, any possession proceedings commenced in reliance upon it might fail as well. (For further details of how to defend possession proceedings, see Chapter 11.)

In addition, if the tenancy is a periodic tenancy, as most council tenancies will be, the notice must also specify the earliest date upon which possession proceedings can be commenced. This cannot be earlier than the date on which the landlord could have brought the tenancy to an end by giving the tenant notice to quit. So in the case of a weekly tenancy this date will be at least four weeks after the notice is given to the tenant, and in the case of a monthly tenancy, at least one month afterwards. The possession proceedings must then be commenced after the date specified, but no more than 12 months from that date. Note that in the case of secure tenants, the landlord does not have to give notice to quit. If a notice of intention to start possession proceedings is received, the next step the landlord is entitled to take is to commence court proceedings against the tenants claiming possession. The tenant will not receive a notice to quit as well.

Orders for possession

The 1985 Housing Act sets out 16 grounds for possession; there are no mandatory grounds. So even if the landlord has followed the correct procedure to establish one of the grounds, there is no certainty that the court will order possession. The nature of the discretion given to the court differs according to the ground proven:

- the court cannot make an order for possession on Grounds 1 to 8 unless it considers it reasonable to do so
- the court cannot make an order for possession on Grounds 9 to 11 unless it is satisfied that suitable alternative accommodation will be available to the tenant when the order takes effect
- the court cannot make an order for possession on Grounds 12 to 16 unless it considers it reasonable to make an order *and* it is satisfied that suitable alternative accommodation will be available when the order takes effect.

Grounds for possession

Ground 1
Rent lawfully due from the tenant has not been paid or some other obligation under the tenancy has not been complied with.

Note that there is no minimum amount of rent which must be due before this ground can be used. It is likely, however, that the amount and frequency of arrears would be relevant factors for the court to consider when deciding whether it is reasonable to order possession.

As to the requirement that the rent must be 'lawfully due', note that the provisions of the Landlord and Tenant Act 1987, which require the landlord to give to the tenant an address in England or Wales at which documents may be served on him, also apply to local authority landlords.

Ground 2

The tenant or a person residing in the house has been guilty of conduct which is a nuisance or annoyance to neighbours, or has been convicted of using the house for an illegal or immoral purpose.

It is not sufficient to show that the house is being used for illegal or immoral purposes: a conviction is necessary. However, illegal or immoral actions may well be a cause of annoyance to neighbours and may be sufficient for possession purposes.

Ground 3

The condition of the house has deteriorated due to the acts or neglect of the tenant or someone residing there. In the case of acts of someone other than the tenant it is also necessary for the landlord to show that the tenant has *not* taken reasonable steps to remove that person from the house.

Ground 4

The condition of the furniture provided by the landlord has deteriorated due to ill-treatment by the tenant or a person residing in the house. In the case of ill-treatment by a person other than the tenant it is also necessary to show that the tenant has not taken reasonable steps to remove that person from the house.

Ground 5

The landlord was induced to grant the tenancy by a false statement made knowingly or recklessly by the tenant.

This ground might be available if, for example, a prospective tenant misrepresented his circumstances to, say, a local authority in order to obtain council accommodation.

Ground 6
The tenancy was assigned to the tenant and a premium was paid in connection with that assignment.

Ground 7
The property let forms part of premises which are not, in the main, used for housing, and the tenant is an employee of the landlord (e.g. a school caretaker living in a house in the grounds of the school), and he or someone living with him, is guilty of conduct which, taking into account the purpose for which the premises are used, means it would not be right for him to continue living there (e.g. a school caretaker found guilty of offences against children).

Ground 8
The house was made available to the tenant whilst his previous house was being repaired and that previous accommodation is now once more available for occupation.

Ground 9
The dwellinghouse is so overcrowded that the occupier is guilty of an offence under the Housing Act 1985.

The definition of overcrowding is complex, but includes situations such as two or more people of different sexes over the age of 10 sharing a room (if they are not living together as husband and wife).

Ground 10
The landlord intends to demolish or reconstruct the house and cannot reasonably do so without obtaining possession.

Ground 10A
The house is within the area of a redevelopment scheme approved by the Secretary of State for such a purpose or the

Housing Corporation and the landlord intends to dispose of the house in accordance with the scheme.

Ground 11
The landlord is a charity and the tenant's continued occupation of the property would conflict with the interests of the charity.

Ground 12
The house forms part of a building which is used mainly for non-housing purposes and the house was let to the tenant by reason of his employment and the landlord now reasonably requires the house for occupation by another person in his employment.

Ground 13
The house contains features designed to make it suitable for physically disabled persons, but there is no longer such a person living in the house and the landlord requires possession for occupation by such a person.

Ground 14
The landlord is a housing association or trust which lets property to persons whose circumstances (other than financial) make it difficult for them to secure housing, but there is no longer such a person living in the house and the landlord requires possession for occupation by such a person.

Ground 15
The house is one of a group of houses let for occupation by persons with special needs, but there is no longer such a person living in the house and the landlord requires possession for occupation by such a person.

Ground 16
The tenancy was created on the death of the previous tenant (with the exception of a spouse), accommodation in the house is more extensive than is reasonably required by him, *and* the notice of proceedings for possession was served

more than six but not more than 12 months after the date of the previous tenant's death.

Succession on the death of a tenant

The tenancy does not end with the death of a secure tenant. If there is a spouse, he or she will succeed to the secure tenancy, provided that he or she was occupying the house as his or her only or principal home at the time of the tenant's death. The definition of spouse includes a person living with the tenant as husband or wife. If there is no 'spouse', a member of the tenant's family who has resided in the house with the tenant *for at least 12 months* prior to the tenant's death will succeed to the tenancy. Note that only one succession is permitted.

If there is no one to succeed to the tenancy, it will pass on death in the same way as the rest of the deceased's property, i.e. either by the deceased's will or according to the rules of intestacy. However, it will no longer be a secure tenancy and so the landlord will be entitled to possession on the termination of the tenancy. Termination will take place under normal common-law rules, e.g. notice to quit in the case of a periodic tenancy. Possession proceedings can then be brought without the need to comply with the secure tenancy procedure, but a court order will still be necessary to enforce the landlord's right to possession.

Assignment of secure tenancies

It is not generally possible to assign a secure tenancy to someone else. If a purported assignment takes place, then the tenancy will cease to be a secure tenancy. However, assignments are permitted in the following circumstances:

- by way of exchange with another secure tenant
- in accordance with a property adjustment order made in matrimonial proceedings
- in accordance with the rules of succession (see above).

Lodgers and subletting

A secure tenant may take in lodgers but may not part with possession or sublet the whole or part of the house without the landlord's written consent. Such consent may not be unreasonably withheld.

If a secure tenant does part with possession or sublets the whole house, then the tenancy will cease to be secure. This means that on the termination of the tenancy, the landlord will be entitled to possession without the need to follow the secure tenancy procedure or to prove secure tenancy grounds.

Rent control

There is no limit on the amount of rent chargeable by a landlord on the grant of a secure tenancy. However, once a tenancy has been granted, the landlord may subsequently increase the rent only if there is a provision in the tenancy agreement permitting this. In the case of periodic tenancies, where there is no such provision, the landlord may serve a notice on the tenant specifying the proposed increase, giving at least four weeks' notice of when the increase is to take effect. A tenant has no right to object to this, nor to refer the matter to an independent assessor.

Tenants' improvements

It is an implied term of every secure tenancy that a tenant may not carry out any improvement, alteration or addition to the property without the landlord's consent. The landlord's consent may not be unreasonably withheld; if it is, then the tenant can proceed as if consent had been given to go ahead without any comeback against him by the landlord. However, tenants should be very wary of judging whether the landlord has been reasonable or not; if it is subsequently adjudged that the landlord *had* been reasonable in withholding his consent, then the tenant will be in breach of his tenancy agreement and possibly liable to possession proceedings as well.

A little-known feature of this requirement is that the landlord's consent is also necessary for the erection of a television aerial or satellite dish. Breach of this term of the tenancy would, in theory at least, leave the tenant open to possession proceedings based on Ground 1 (see page 86), although it is questionable whether it would ever be reasonable to order possession in such a situation.

Repairs

Repairs to council houses and other secure tenancies are governed by the same provisions that apply to other tenancies (see Chapter 8). In the vast majority of cases the landlord is responsible for repairs to the structure and exterior of the property and for keeping in repair and proper working order the facilities in the house for the supply of gas and electricity, room and water heating and sanitation.

The right to buy

Perhaps the most valuable right that a secure tenant has is the right to buy the freehold in his house, or, in the case of a flat, to acquire a 125-year lease of it. Since its introduction in 1980, the right-to-buy scheme has been enormously popular and has been exercised by over a million council tenants. However, in order to claim this right the tenant must, as well as being a secure tenant, satisfy a residence qualification, which requires that the tenant (or his spouse) must have resided in public-sector accommodation for at least two years. Note that he need not be a secure tenant, nor need he have always been in the same premises, nor in the premises which he now wishes to purchase.

Price of freehold

The price is to be the open-market value of the property, but is subject to a substantial discount in recognition of the length of time that the tenant has spent in public-sector accommodation. In order to encourage flat tenants to buy, local authorities offer greater discounts on flat purchases than on houses.

Every house purchase is subject to a minimum discount of

32 per cent of the open-market value, plus a further 1 per cent discount for every complete year for which the residence qualification has been satisfied – up to a maximum of 60 per cent. A flat purchase is subject to a minimum discount of 44 per cent plus a further 2 per cent for each complete year of residence, with a maximum discount of 70 per cent. The discount is limited in all cases to a maximum of £50,000.

Initially the local authority specifies what it considers to be the market value of the property. If the tenant considers the price too high, he has the right to appeal to the District Valuer within three months. The District Valuer's decision is final.

Repayment of discount

The tenant must repay some or all of the discount to the landlord if he sells the property within three years of buying it. This is to stop people from buying property cheaply and then making a large profit on the resale. So, if the tenant resells within one year, he must repay 100 per cent of the discount; if he resells between one and two years after the purchase, he must repay 66 per cent of the discount, and if he sells between two and three years after the purchase, he must repay 33 per cent of the discount. After three years, no repayment of the discount is required. A gift of the property can be made at any time, even within three years of purchase, and it can pass on death without the need for repayment of the discount.

The right to buy on rent-to-mortgage terms

Despite the popularity of the right-to-buy provisions, it is the Government's belief that there are still many secure tenants who would like to buy their council houses, but are unable to afford to do so. The right to buy on rent-to-mortgage terms has therefore been introduced to enable the less well-off to buy their council houses.

The idea behind the scheme is quite simple: a secure tenant who has the right to buy should be able to buy the house without it costing him any more per month than he is presently paying in rent to the council. Unfortunately, the scheme's operation is quite complicated, as the tenant is required to serve a number of notices on the landlord to exercise his right to buy. Help with these forms is available from local authority housing departments.

Assuming that he is a secure tenant with a right to buy, the tenant approaches any mortgage lender – a bank or building society – and makes an initial payment to the landlord. This payment need be no more than the amount which would be advanced on a 25-year ordinary repayment mortgage, with repayments at the same level as the rent currently being paid. So instead of paying, say, £30 per week in rent, the buyer will now be paying that amount in mortgage repayments.

Although this initial payment may well be a comparatively small amount, the ownership of the freehold will still be transferred to the tenant immediately; he does not have to wait until the full purchase price has been paid. However, the landlord does still own a 'share' in the house, secured by a second mortgage which he organises. However, no repayments will have to be made on this second mortgage, and the sum due to the landlord will not be liable to any interest. It is, in effect, an interest-free loan from the landlord, and will have to be paid off only on a subsequent disposal of the house, or upon the tenant/mortgagor's death. The tenant should have no problem repaying the loan should he sell the house, but the provision that it must be repaid on the death of the tenant may cause problems for surviving relatives if they need to live in the house but do not have enough money to make the repayment. In such a situation, the landlord would be entitled to force a sale of the house to recover his money. This can be avoided if the tenant ensures that his life insurance policy is sufficient to cover the mortgage.

Q *I have a tenancy of a council house. My house needed a lot of work doing to it so the council has put me in another house temporarily. This is in a much nicer area. Where we were before there was a lot of drug-taking and my 5-year-old child frequently found discarded needles in the garden. Do I have to go back to the old house?*

A Possibly. Otherwise, the council could try to get a possession order against you using Ground 8. However, the court can only order possession if it thinks it reasonable to do so. You would have to try to argue that, due to the circumstances outlined, it was not. In the event of an order for possession being made against you, it is unlikely that you would be made homeless, as your local authority would be obliged to find you accommodation. Because you have a young child, you would be classed as a priority need, and the most likely outcome is that you would be rehoused in your former home. You should discuss your worries with the housing department and your local councillor without delay.

Q *I have a council flat. Am I allowed to keep a dog?*

A There is nothing in the Housing Act 1985 dealing with this question: it depends upon the terms of your tenancy agreement. Flat tenancy agreements frequently prohibit the keeping of dogs and if yours does you would put yourself in breach of your tenancy agreement if you were to do so, which would entitle the council to bring eviction proceedings against you. If there is no such prohibition in your tenancy agreement you may keep a dog.

Q *I have a council house. As I am short of cash, may I take in a student from the nearby college to earn some extra money?*

A Yes. Notwithstanding the terms of your tenancy agreement, you have a right to take in a lodger. What you must not do, however, is let all or part of your house. This would be in breach of the terms of your tenancy and the council would be entitled to bring possession proceedings against you.

CHAPTER 7

HOUSING ASSOCIATIONS

A HOUSING association is a non-profit making body established to provide affordable accommodation. Such organisations have existed in one form or another since the mid-nineteenth century, but their number has grown considerably since the introduction of state-funded housing associations in the 1960s. Most local authorities, housing advice centres and Citizens Advice Bureaux will provide a list of properties available locally.

Housing associations are now one of the major providers of state-funded housing. Some of them are registered with the Housing Corporation or with Housing for Wales and are called registered housing associations. (The Housing Corporation has responsibility for England; Housing for Wales is the government body responsible in the principality.) Some housing associations (but by no means all) are also registered as charities and must therefore operate within their own charitable rules as well. Other housing associations are run on a co-operative basis where the tenants themselves own and manage the houses they live in. The law relating to security of tenure and rent control will depend not only on the type of housing association, but also on the date when the tenancy was granted: tenancies entered into before 15 January 1989 are dealt with differently from tenancies granted on or after that date.

Registered housing associations

Tenancies granted on or after 15 January 1989

The Housing Act 1988 brought registered housing association tenancies into the private sector. Therefore, these tenants will have either an assured tenancy or an assured shorthold tenancy under the Act (see Chapters 2 and 3). Most of these will be ordinary assured tenancies rather than assured shorthold tenancies, although there is no legal rule prohibiting a housing association from granting an assured shorthold tenancy if it sees fit to do so.

Assured tenants have security of tenure in that the landlord must prove a statutory ground for possession under the 1988 Act if it wishes to evict one of its tenants (see pages 24–33). Tenants should be aware, however, that there is legal control over rent increases even though one of the reasons for having a housing association is to create lettings at affordable rents. Registered housing associations should provide their tenants with a written agreement specifying the level of rents to be charged and the conditions of the tenancy. Tenants also have the benefit of a 'tenant's guarantee', which is an assurance from the landlord of good standards of management. Although not legally binding, the guarantee specifies the minimum contractual rights a tenant should be given in his tenancy agreement with regard to taking in lodgers, carrying out improvements, etc.

It also contains information on:

- the association's policies for selecting tenants and allocating homes
- rents (which should be kept within the reach of people in low-paid or no employment)
- management, maintenance and tenant participation.

Tenancies resulting from a transfer from a local authority

Former tenants of public landlords where the property has been transferred to a registered housing association on or after 15 January 1989 will normally become assured tenants under the Housing Act 1988 (see Chapter 2). However, such tenants retain their right to buy (see page 92) and this is enforceable against the new landlord. This is known as 'the preserved right to buy'.

Tenancies granted before 15 January 1989

Before 15 January 1989, housing association tenancies were treated, in the main, as being in the public sector and therefore the rules relating to secure tenancies apply, including the right to buy. Unlike public-sector tenancies, however, the fair rent system also applies (see page 60).

Unregistered housing associations

An unregistered housing association is one that has not registered with the Housing Corporation or Housing for Wales. This means it does not qualify for state funding and is not supervised by a government body. Some housing associations have deliberately chosen not to be registered but prefer to act independently so that the members can set up shared-ownership schemes, not possible with a registered association.

Tenancies granted on or after 15 January 1989

These tenancies will be assured tenancies or assured shorthold tenancies under the Housing Act 1988. They are governed by the same rules regarding security of tenure and rent control as private sector tenancies. They do not, however, have the benefit of the 'tenant's guarantee' (see above).

Tenancies granted before 15 January 1989

Unregistered housing association tenancies granted before this date will come under the protection of the Rent Act 1977 as regards both security of tenure and rent control (see Chapter 4).

Co-operative housing associations

Tenancies granted before 15 January 1989

Co-operative housing association tenancies granted prior to this date enjoy no statutory security of tenure. The security therefore depends on the terms of the tenancy agreement. However, since the tenants are in effect their own landlords, with their own co-operative constitution, they should be reasonably protected.

The fair rent system applies (see page 60) and therefore a registered rent is the maximum that can be charged.

Tenancies granted on or after 15 January 1989

A fully mutual housing association is exempt from the Housing Act 1988 and therefore the tenant will have no statutory protection apart from what is stated in the tenancy agreement. However, the tenant's guarantee applies (see page 98), which gives the tenant some measure of protection.

Q *I was a council tenant for many years but in 1993 the ownership of my flat was transferred to a registered housing association. Has this affected my legal rights?*

A You are now an assured rather than a secure tenant, and your landlord should have informed you of how this change would affect you before it took place. In fact, your new status should have very little effect on your rights, as the landlord is still unable to evict you without proving a ground for possession, you still have no protection against rent increases, and you retain the right to buy your home.

Q *I am a tenant of a housing association. I am worried that the landlord never gets round to doing any repairs. What is my legal position on this?*

A Your landlord has exactly the same repairing obligations as any private landlord. If you have a periodic tenancy or a fixed-term tenancy of less than seven years, you should enforce these obligations without delay (see Chapter 8).

Q *Is there any legal limit on the amount of rent which a housing association can charge?*

A In the case of housing association tenancies granted before 15 January 1989 the 'fair rent' system, whereby a maximum rent is fixed by a rent officer, will apply. Tenancies granted after this date will usually be governed by the Housing Act 1988 and rental values are not controlled by law. However, registered housing associations have a 'tenant's guarantee' which, although not legally binding, states that rents should be kept within the reach of people in low-paid employment.

CHAPTER **8**

REPAIR AND MAINTENANCE OF RENTED PROPERTY

ONE OF the major hazards when renting or letting property is the question of maintenance and repair. Who is to be responsible if the roof starts leaking, the central heating system breaks down, or if someone is injured after tripping on a broken path or garden steps? Even if the landlord and tenant have a comprehensive tenancy agreement that covers these matters in full (which is rare in any event), various Acts of Parliament often overrule what the parties have actually agreed. To make matters worse, the law is not contained in any one single statute: it is a mixture of common law (judge-made law) and various statutory provisions designed to deal with diverse matters.

EXAMPLE

Bleak House is a large Victorian house divided into two flats. The ground-floor flat is occupied by tenant A, the top-floor flat by tenant B. The ground-floor flat is let on a five-year lease but under the terms of the lease the tenant has an option to renew for a further five years. The top-floor flat is let on a monthly periodic tenancy. Both tenants have undertaken to keep the property in a good state of repair.

The large attic is retained by the landlord and used for storage purposes. There is a shared front door and the staircase is used by tenant B to gain access to the top-floor flat and by the landlord to gain access to the attic. There is a communal boiler in the basement (retained by the

landlord) which supplies hot water and central heating to both flats; it often breaks down. There is rising damp in the ground-floor flat because there is no damp-proof course, and penetrating damp in the top-floor flat because the gutters and downspouts are defective and the brickwork needs repointing. Both flats are affected by condensation because of the lack of ventilation and their wallpaper is peeling. The window frames are rotten and could do with replacing. The roof is also in a poor condition.

Who is liable for these defects?

An overview of the law

In common law landlord/tenant liability for repairs is governed by the tenancy agreement. The tenancy between the landlord and the tenant is a form of contract. The terms of that contract may be set out expressly (express terms) or may be implied by law (implied terms). Some of these implied terms are implied by common law, others by Acts of Parliament known as statutory implied terms. The common law implied terms can be overridden by express terms of the tenancy agreement but the statutory implied terms cannot generally be ousted by the tenancy agreement, which makes the statutory implied terms extremely important.

It is therefore necessary to look at:

- the express terms of the tenancy agreement
- the common law implied terms (but bearing in mind that these can be excluded if the tenancy agreement says otherwise)
- the statutory implied terms (bearing in mind that these cannot normally be excluded and will therefore operate despite the terms of the tenancy agreement).

Breach of these express or implied terms is a breach of contract and can be enforced only by the parties to the contract i.e. the landlord or the tenant as the case may be. They cannot be enforced by third parties, such as members of the tenant's family, any visitors to the property or the local authority.

However, quite apart from the express or implied terms of the tenancy, the Environmental Protection Act 1990 gives the local authority wide powers of intervention to deal with premises which create a 'statutory nuisance', e.g. where the premises are a danger to health (see page 115). Enforcement of the Environmental Protection Act is in the hands of the local authority which, if necessary, may bring a prosecution in the magistrates' court. In certain circumstances, such as where the landlord is itself a local authority, the tenant can take direct action under the Act. Local authorities also have wide additional powers to deal with 'unfit houses' under the Housing Act 1985.

Finally, if someone is injured as a result of defective premises the injured party may be able to bring an action for damages for breach of the Occupiers' Liability Act 1957 or the Defective Premises Act 1972. In such a case, the claim would be for negligence and a claim for monetary compensation could be pursued through the civil courts. This is of course not a direct method of getting the defects put right.

These matters are examined in more detail below, in the context of the problems facing tenants A and B at Bleak House.

The tenancy agreement

The tenancy agreement may set out clauses which stipulate who is liable for what repair. If the landlord has undertaken to do all the repairs the tenant can enforce these obligations – through the courts if necessary. The landlord's liability will depend upon the precise wording of the relevant clauses. However, even if the tenancy agreement does say that the landlord is liable for repairs it does not necessarily follow that the landlord will be liable for *all* the matters about which the tenant complains.

'Repair' must be distinguished from 'improvement'. The word 'repair' is confined to the renewal or replacement of subsidiary parts of the building; improvement is adding things to the property that do not already exist. The law does not impose an obligation on the landlord to effect improvements unless (and this would be most unusual) he has expressly agreed to do so.

The dampness at Bleak House caused by leaking gutters and brickwork that needs repointing would be classed as repairs and the landlord would be liable to do this work if he has undertaken to carry out repairs. However, putting in an entirely new damp course (Bleak House does not have one to repair) would probably be classed as an improvement. Similarly, curing the condensation may involve putting in new windows or a new type of heating system, which, again, would probably be considered an improvement, not a repair.

If the terms of the tenancy agreement place the repairing obligation on the tenants the question of whether or not this would be enforceable depends on the length of the tenancy and the type of repairs in question. If a tenant has a periodic tenancy (like tenant B at Bleak House) or a fixed-term tenancy for less than seven years, most of the major repairing obligations will be placed on the landlord by virtue of Section 11 of the Landlord and Tenant Act 1985 (see page 108). Tenant A at Bleak House is not covered by Section 11 as his five-year lease contains a five-year renewal option, thus exceeding the seven-year limit.

The tenancy agreement may stipulate that the tenant is liable for internal decorative repairs. Quite often, however, the tenancy agreement is silent on this matter, in which case one must look to the implied terms arising either at common law or under statute.

Common law implied terms

Unfortunately, the common law is of little assistance in the vast majority of cases: if the tenancy agreement is silent, the general rule is that there is no implication that the premises are fit for human habitation or that either party will be responsible for repairs. In other words, the common law is largely neutral. However, there are some minor exceptions which are explained below.

Furnished lettings

In the case of a furnished letting the landlord warrants (by implication) that the property is fit for habitation at the date when the tenancy commences. Therefore, if a furnished house is uninhabitable because it is infested with bugs the tenant can, at the start of the tenancy, immediately repudiate the tenancy, recover any deposit or rent that he has paid and sue the landlord for any damage or loss suffered. However, the tenant must act quickly since this implied term arises only at the commencement of the tenancy. The landlord cannot be compelled to make the property habitable. The tenant's remedy is simply to cancel the agreement and recover his losses. There is no continuing obligation on the part of the landlord to keep the furnished premises fit for habitation.

Tenant's duty to use the property in a tenant-like manner

There is no implied term in any tenancy agreement, whether of a furnished or unfurnished property, that the tenant is to be responsible for repairs. However, the tenant must use the property in a 'tenant-like manner'. This means that he must take proper care of the property by doing the little jobs which can reasonably be expected of him, such as unblocking drains, cleaning chimneys, mending fuses, etc.

Common parts

In certain circumstances where a tenancy agreement is signed but is incomplete, the court may imply a term, at common law, that the landlord will take reasonable care of common parts, e.g. staircases and other facilities which are shared between various tenants. If the premises consist of a large tower block containing lifts, staircases and other common parts and the tenancy agreements of the individual flats do not oblige either tenant or landlord to maintain the common parts, the court may hold that, since the agreement is incomplete and the premises cannot function without such common parts being maintained, the landlord must have taken responsibility by implication to keep them in a reasonable condition. This could help tenants A and B if, for example, the shared staircase became dangerous to use. However, the tenants would probably be better advised to look to the statutory implied terms.

Statutory implied terms

These are to be found in the Landlord and Tenant Act 1985. The most important provisions are contained in Section 11, but if the lease or tenancy is at a very low rent the tenant may also find assistance in Section 8 (see page 111).

Section 11 of the Landlord and Tenant Act 1985

Section 11 applies to leases or tenancies granted on or after 24 October 1961 for less than seven years. The expression 'for less than seven years' can, however, be misleading, since Section 11 applies to *all* periodic tenancies even if the tenant is there for longer than seven years, but if the lease is for a fixed term of seven years or longer, Section 11 will not apply. Moreover, Section 11 will not apply if the fixed term was originally granted for less than seven years and the tenant was also granted an option to extend the lease which, if exercised, would take the lease beyond the seven-year limit (as with tenant A at Bleak House).

The vast majority of residential tenancies are, however, periodic or for terms of less than seven years, therefore Section 11 will apply in most cases, including that of tenant B.

The landlord's implied obligations under Section 11 are:

- to keep in repair the structure and exterior of the dwelling (including drains, gutters and external pipes)
- to keep in repair and proper working order the installations in the dwelling for the supply of water, gas, electricity and sanitation (including basins, sinks, baths and sanitary conveniences)
- to keep in repair and proper working order the installations in the dwelling for room and water heating.

'Structure and exterior' in the first point are not defined by the Act. However, 'structure' clearly includes the main fabric of the dwelling such as the main walls, foundations and roof timbers (including window frames) as distinct from decorations and fittings, while 'exterior' has been held by the courts to include paths or steps which form an essential means of access to the dwelling but not paving in the backyard or a footpath at the rear of the house.

The words 'structure' and 'exterior' can cause particular problems where a property is divided into flats. The courts have held that the landlord's implied obligation extends only to the particular flat in question and not to the entire building. Therefore, it would not extend to the roof or common parts which do not physically form part of one or other of the flats. On this interpretation, tenants A and B of Bleak House would have great difficulty in arguing that the roof or the staircase forms part of their individual flats. New legislation was brought in by the Housing Act 1988 but only in respect of leases or tenancies granted on or after 15 January 1989. Under this legislation the landlord's obligations under Section 11 are deemed to include parts of the building belonging to the same landlord or which are under the landlord's control. However, this extended obligation will apply only where the disrepair affects the tenant's enjoyment of the flat or common parts in question.

For tenant B of Bleak House the extension of the legislation is a welcome improvement. It means the landlord can be held liable for repairs to the roof if it is the cause of damp in the flat. The same applies to the gutters and drains.

The condensation, however, remains a problem, as the landlord is only obliged to carry out 'repairs'. If the condensation has caused damage to the main fabric of the property, such as the plasterwork, the landlord could be made to repair the plasterwork, but this will not cure the condensation; it will simply repair the *consequences* of condensation. If the condensation cannot be cured by 'repair' but can only be eradicated by 'improvements', the landlord is not liable under Section 11 to remedy the problem. To get rid of the condensation tenants A and B may well have to invoke the Environmental Protection Act 1990 (see pages 114–16).

The landlord's obligations to repair and keep in proper working order the installations for the supply of water, gas, electricity, sanitation, room and water heating merely require him to maintain and repair the facilities that exist at the *start* of the tenancy. If the dwelling does not have these facilities to begin with, then there is no obligation on the part of the landlord to provide the necessary installations.

Originally, the legislation was confined to installations which were actually within the four walls of the dwelling. If, as at Bleak House, there is a communal central heating boiler in the basement serving both flats the landlord would not, originally, have been liable under Section 11 to repair that boiler since it was not within either flat. However, if the tenancy was granted on or after 15 January 1989 the landlord would be liable for the boiler irrespective of where it was located.

The landlord is liable for these matters even if the problem is a manufacturing defect, e.g. if the boiler was defective when it was supplied and fitted. He has to put the problem right even if it was not his fault: this is known as strict liability (the landlord may none the less have rights under the Sale of Goods Act 1979 or the Supply of Goods and Services Act 1982 in respect of the faulty boiler). The only exception would be where the defect is due to some fault on the part of the tenants, who must use the property in a 'tenant-like manner' (see page 107). So if the problems arise because the tenants have not used the property in a tenant-like manner, the landlord is not liable for repairs to the items in question.

Standards of repair

Section 11 provides that in determining the standards of repair to the property the courts must have regard to the character and prospective lifespan of the property and the locality in which it is situated. Therefore, if the house is in a poor condition at the start of the tenancy and in an area of very poor-quality housing the landlord will not have to carry out comprehensive repairs under Section 11, nor will he be obliged to carry out improvements. Patching repairs may satisfy the requirements of Section 11, depending upon the circumstances of the case.

Exceptions to section 11

Some specific situations are *not* covered by Section 11. These are:

- repairs for which the tenant is liable by virtue of his duty to use the premises in a tenant-like manner (see above)

- re-building or reinstating the premises in case of damage or destruction by fire, tempest or other accident
- keeping in repair or maintaining anything that the tenant is entitled to remove from the dwelling when he leaves (tenant's fixtures).

The requirement for notice

The landlord is not liable under Section 11 (or indeed under any of the express or implied obligations) unless the tenant has given him notice of the need for repair. So, if a tenant is injured as a result of a defect, the landlord will not be liable for his injuries if he had not been notified of the need to repair the defect. Tenants should, therefore, inform their landlord as soon as they are aware that a problem exists. The notice does not have to be in any particular form, nor does it necessarily have to come from the tenant. A letter from the local authority, from a surveyor or from the landlord's agent would also be sufficient to put the landlord on notice.

Section 8 of the Landlord and Tenant Act 1985

If the dwelling has been let at a very low rent, not exceeding £80 in London or £52 per annum elsewhere, the landlord has an additional obligation: namely, that the house is fit for human habitation at the start of the tenancy and will be kept in that condition throughout the tenancy. (Few properties fall into this category, for obvious reasons.)

Landlord's right of access to carry out repairs

Normally the tenancy agreement will expressly allow the landlord to enter the property for the purpose of inspection and carrying out repairs. If not, the landlord also has a right of entry if the tenancy is governed by the Rent Act 1977 (see Chapter 4) or the Housing Act 1988 (see Chapter 2). In any event, where the landlord is obliged to carry out repairs under Section 11 of the Landlord and Tenant Act 1985 he may, on giving 24 hours' notice in writing, enter the property to inspect its condition and state of repair.

Remedies for breaches of the landlord's repairing obligations

The repairing obligations mentioned above are part of the express or implied terms of the tenancy contract, and therefore only the tenant can enforce them. If the landlord fails to meet his obligations, the tenant has a number of remedies available to him, outlined below:

* he could sue the landlord through the courts for an order known as 'specific performance' which compels the landlord to carry out the specified repairs
* if he has already done the repairs he could recover the cost by making a claim for damages. Damages could also be claimed for the cost of finding alternative accommodation while the repairs were being carried out, assuming that the property was unfit for habitation during this period
* he could opt for a 'self-help' scheme whereby notice of the need for repairs is given to the landlord and he is allowed a reasonable time in which to carry them out.

The problem with the first option – the order known as 'specific performance' – is that this is a discretionary remedy and can only be obtained through litigation. The 'self-help' scheme is therefore preferable wherever possible.

Under this scheme, it is possible in certain circumstances for the tenant to have the work done and to deduct the cost of the work from rent due to the landlord or from future rent. This option will be feasible only if the cost of repairs is within the tenant's own means and the rent is sufficiently high for the tenant to be able to recoup the amount spent over a reasonable period. It is advisable for the tenant to obtain at least three estimates for the cost of the work and to submit copies of these estimates to the landlord together with a letter informing him that if he does not carry out the work by a certain date (which must give the landlord reasonable time), the tenant proposes to have the work done and to deduct the cost from the rent which would otherwise be due.

The self-help remedy should be used only if the landlord is clearly in breach and the repairs are clearly the landlord's responsibility: if there is any doubt about the matter the tenant should not pursue this option, since the erroneous withholding of rent by the tenant could render him liable to being sued by the landlord for possession on the grounds of rent arrears.

In the Bleak House example one of the clear breaches by the landlord was his failure to mend the leaking gutters. If the landlord, having been given notice, fails to repair these gutters within a reasonable time, it would be appropriate for the tenants to obtain estimates for the work themselves, forward them to the landlord and tell him that they propose to have the work done if the landlord fails to carry out the work within, say, four weeks. The tenants could then deduct the cost by withholding rent.

This self-help scheme is available to all residential tenants whose landlord is clearly in breach of a landlord's repairing obligation. Secure tenants in the public sector have a special scheme, described immediately below.

Secure tenancies (right-to-repair scheme) regulations 1985

Since 1 January 1986 public sector secure tenants (with the exception of tenants of co-operative housing associations) have been able to use a special statutory procedure, set out in the right-to-repair scheme regulations. The scheme is limited to 'qualifying repairs', which means any repairs for which the landlord is responsible other than repairs to the structure and exterior of a flat. Under the scheme, the tenant must first serve notice on the landlord describing the proposed works, why they are needed and the materials to be used. The landlord must then reply within 21 days, either granting or refusing the tenant's repair claim. The landlord *may* refuse the claim in the following circumstances:

- where the landlord's costs would be more than £200
- where the landlord intends to carry out the work within 28 days of the claim
- where the works are not reasonably necessary for the personal comfort or safety of the tenant and those living with him and

the landlord intends to carry them out within one year as part of a planned programme of repair

- where the works would infringe the terms of any guarantee of which the landlord has the benefit
- where the tenant has unreasonably failed to provide the landlord with access for inspection.

The landlord *must* refuse the claim in the following circumstances:

- where the landlord's costs would be less than £20
- where works do not constitute qualifying repairs
- where the works, if carried out using the materials specified, would not in the landlord's opinion satisfactorily remedy the problem.

Because of these conditions many tenants choose not to use the statutory scheme but to reply upon the common law rules mentioned in the previous section (pages 112–3).

The Environmental Protection Act 1990

As an alternative to suing privately to make the landlord do the repairs a tenant may enlist the assistance of the local authority under Sections 79–82 of the Environmental Protection Act 1990. This legislation is concerned primarily with public health and is designed to prevent what is termed 'statutory nuisance'. This is defined in Section 79 to include, amongst other things, 'any premises in such a state as to be prejudicial to health or a nuisance'.

If a local authority is satisfied that a statutory nuisance exists then it must serve an abatement notice on the appropriate person (usually the landlord) requiring work to be carried out to 'abate the nuisance'. Not complying with an abatement notice is an offence, for which the landlord could be prosecuted in the magistrates' court. If the prosecution is successful, the tenant may be eligible to apply for a compensation order against the landlord for loss or damage arising from the offence committed.

Prejudicial to health

A statutory nuisance arises if the premises are, because of disrepair or other reason, injurious or likely to cause injury to health. Therefore, if it can be shown that the premises are in such a condition that a person living there who is normally in good health is likely to become ill or that a sick person's health is likely to deteriorate further because of the condition of the premises, a statutory nuisance exists.

Damp, condensation, defective plasterwork, broken glass, dangerous gas and electrical installations may all constitute statutory nuisances, but the evidence of an environmental health officer who has inspected the premises will be required as grounds for an abatement notice.

A nuisance

A 'nuisance' means either a public nuisance or a private nuisance at common law. Public nuisance consists of an act or omission which adversely affects the comfort and quality of life for the public generally or a particular class of citizens. Public nuisance is unlikely to be relevant in the context of tenancies. Private nuisance is a substantial interference by the owner or occupier of a property with the use or enjoyment of neighbouring property. So if a landlord retains common parts or adjoining or neighbouring premises and the common parts or the neighbouring premises are in disrepair and this leads to interference with the tenanted property, e.g. water penetration, this may constitute a statutory nuisance for the purposes of the Act.

Tenants can therefore ask the local authority to intervene if the condition of the property makes it prejudicial to the occupants' health or a nuisance exists caused by defects in other premises owned by the landlord. If the local authority is satisfied that a statutory nuisance exists, it must serve an abatement notice requiring work to be carried out to prevent the nuisance occurring or recurring. The notice will specify what work has to be done. If the notice is not complied with the local authority may bring a prosecution, but this would be a criminal proceeding, in which the case against the landlord must be proved beyond reasonable doubt.

If the local authority is also the landlord, and the tenant wishes to use the Environmental Protection Act, the procedure described above is clearly inappropriate as the local authority cannot take proceedings against itself. The tenant may therefore use an alternative procedure laid down in Section 82 of the Act. This requires the tenant to make a complaint to a local magistrates' court, which, if satisfied that a statutory nuisance exists, may require the local authority to abate the nuisance within a specified time and, failing compliance, to impose a fine. It should be noted that legal aid is not available for proceedings under the Environmental Protection Act.

Houses unfit for human habitation: Housing Act 1985

If the property is in such bad condition that it is unfit for human habitation, the local authority has wide powers to deal with the situation under Part VI of the Housing Act 1985.

The Act defines fitness for habitation in negative terms: a house is deemed to be fit for human habitation *unless*, in the opinion of the local authority, it fails to meet certain criteria such as:

- it is structurally stable
- it is free from serious disrepair
- it is free from damp that is prejudicial to the health of the occupants
- it has adequate provision for lighting, heating and ventilation
- it has an adequate pipe supply of good-quality water
- it contains satisfactory facilities for food preparation including a sink with hot and cold running water
- it has suitable WC facilities
- it has a suitable fixed bath or shower and hand basin and a satisfactory supply of hot and cold running water
- it has an effective drainage system.

If a house does not meet the above criteria it may be judged unfit for human habitation.

Local authorities have a duty to consider what action should be taken regarding housing in their area. Normally, a visit from an environmental health officer would be a prerequisite for any action taken under the 1985 Act. Possible courses of action are listed below.

Repair notice

The first option is to carry out repairs and improvements to render the property fit for human habitation. In this case, the local authority must serve a notice on the landlord or managing agent (normally) requiring certain work to be carried out. The recipient has the right to appeal against the notice within 21 days. Subject to an appeal, if the notice is not complied with the local authority may enter and carry out the work itself (but it cannot be compelled to do so) and may charge the cost to the landlord (or managing agent); otherwise, it may institute criminal proceedings against the landlord.

Closing order

The second option is a closing order. This means that the property may not be used for habitation whilst the order remains in force.

Demolition order

The third option is a demolition order requiring the owner to demolish the property and clear the site. If the order is not complied with the local authority has powers to act in default. Again, there is a right of appeal.

Clearance area

If the whole area comprises unfit houses the local authority may declare a clearance area. The result will be the compulsory acquisition of all the relevant properties and the rehousing of the tenants.

Fit houses in need of repair (Section 190, Housing Act 1985)

If a house is fit for human habitation but is in need of substantial repairs to bring it up to a reasonable standard, the local authority may serve a repairs notice on the landlord requiring specified work to be done. This also applies where the condition of the premises is such as to interfere materially with the personal comfort of the tenant. If the notice is not complied with the local authority may do the work itself or commence criminal proceedings.

Q *I rent a house from a private landlord on a monthly tenancy. The property is old and in need of repair but my landlord refuses to do any work. It needs a new damp-proof course since the existing one does not work and the wallpaper in the front room is peeling off. What are my rights?*

A Assuming your tenancy was granted on or after 24 October 1961, your periodic tenancy is covered by Section 11 of the Landlord and Tenant Act 1985. Your landlord is therefore legally responsible for maintaining the structure and mending the damp-proof course. You should write to your landlord telling him that if he does not carry out the work you will sue him for damages or for an order compelling him to carry out the work (or both). Damages would include the cost of repapering the room (and repair to any plasterwork) and also general damages for the inconvenience you have suffered.

Alternatively, if you can afford to have the work done yourself, you should obtain three estimates for the work and send these to your landlord telling him that if he does not do the work, you will. You can then recover the cost by withholding rent.

Another possible course of action is to contact your local authority's environmental health department; it will intervene if the damp is so bad that your health is likely to be affected.

Q *I am a council tenant and want to know how I can insist that the landlord carries out essential repairs. Despite my letters of complaint, no action has been taken.*

A If the repairs relate to the structure and exterior of the property you could use Section 11 of the Landlord and Tenant Act 1985 (legal aid may be available for this). If the house is unhealthy to live in you could threaten to take the local authority to court under the Environmental Protection Act 1990. To do this, however, you will need the evidence of an independent environmental health consultant (legal aid is *not* available for this). Depending on how much the repairs will cost, you could use one of the 'self-help' schemes (provided you obtain estimates first and give the landlord notice of your intentions).

Q *My son was injured after tripping on a broken staircase leading to my rented flat. Can he claim compensation?*

A Your son cannot himself sue the landlord for breach of the tenancy agreement but you may be able to sue on his behalf. In addition, if negligence by the landlord can be established, your son may be able to make a claim for his injuries. If you want to force the landlord to repair the staircase, you may need to take court proceedings for 'specific performance' of his obligations under the express or implied terms of the tenancy agreement.

Q *I am a landlord and recently granted an assured shorthold tenancy for six months. The tenant has given me a letter demanding that I sort out the condensation problem in the house. This is a long-standing problem which dates back to the construction of the house in the 1960s. It is not my fault and can only be solved by virtually rebuilding the place. Am I liable?*

A The tenancy is covered by Section 11 of the Landlord and Tenant Act 1988 and therefore you have responsibility for structural 'repairs'; if the condensation is not caused by disrepair you may not be directly liable to rectify the problem. However, if the condensation has caused damage to the fabric of the property you may be liable for this. If the tenant enlists the help of the local authority under the Environmental Protection Act 1990 and it is found that the condensation poses a health risk, you could be made liable or face a fine.

CHAPTER 9

HARASSMENT AND UNLAWFUL EVICTION

AMONG the most traumatic experiences that a residential tenant or licensee may have to face are harassment and peremptory eviction. Landlords sometimes resort to threats and violence because they see these as cheaper, easier and quicker methods of eviction than taking court proceedings for possession with no guarantee of success.

Tenants who suffer at the hands of their landlords in this way may have civil remedies as well as criminal sanctions available to them.

The tenant's basic remedies are damages, i.e. compensation for the loss suffered, or an injunction, i.e. a court order compelling the landlord to refrain from such actions in the future and to restore the dispossessed tenant to the property. These statutory protections apply not only to tenants but also to licensees, although there is a category of licences and tenancies for which protection is more limited. Apart from these excluded tenancies (see pages 125–6), the protections will apply whether or not the tenant has security of tenure.

Criminal sanctions

The Protection from Eviction Act 1977

This Act imposes criminal penalties in cases of harassment and unlawful eviction. Criminal proceedings may result in the landlord being imprisoned or fined; compensation for the tenant may also be available. Details of offences under the Act are outlined below.

Protection from eviction

It is an offence to evict a residential occupier without a court order unless it is reasonably believed that he no longer lives in the premises.

A residential occupier is defined as someone who occupies the premises as a residence and includes all tenants, whether they are protected tenants under the Rent Act 1977, assured or assured shorthold tenants under the Housing Act 1988, or whether they have no statutory protection at all. Contractual licensees are also included within the definition.

Protection from harassment

Actions by a landlord which would amount to harassment include removing doors and windows, disconnecting services and acts and threats of violence.

There are two offences of harassment: one requires intent on the part of the offender and is set out in Section 1(3); the other is contained in Section 1(3A) and requires only knowledge or belief.

Section 1(3) harassment

It is an offence to commit acts likely to interfere with the peace or comfort of a residential occupier or to withhold services reasonably required for the occupation of the premises with intent to cause the residential occupier to give up the occupation of the premises. The need to *prove* that the landlord intended to cause the occupier to leave can cause problems. What if the landlord says he never intended that to happen? Generally, intent can only be presumed if the particular result was foreseeable as a natural consequence of the actions in question.

Section 1(3A) harassment

It is an offence for a landlord to commit acts likely to interfere with the peace and comfort of a residential occupier, or to withhold services reasonably required for the occupation of the premises, if he knows or has reasonable cause to believe that such conduct is likely to cause the residential occupier to give up the occupation of the premises.

As no proof of specific intention is required for this offence it may well be easier to establish than Section 1(3): this was certainly the intention of the legislature.

The Criminal Law Act 1977

Under Section 6(2) of the Criminal Law Act 1977 it is an offence for anyone 'without lawful authority' to use, or threaten to use, violence to secure entry to premises if there is someone on those premises at the time who is opposed to the entry.

The police are responsible for prosecutions against a landlord under the Criminal Law Act, whereas the local authority will normally bring proceedings under the Protection from Eviction Act. A private prosecution is also possible if the responsible authority refuses to bring proceedings.

Compensation in criminal proceedings

Under Section 35 of the Powers of the Criminal Courts Act 1973, magistrates have the power to order compensation for personal injury, loss or damage resulting from an offence. Compensation is available in relation to all the above offences regardless of who brings the prosecution. If compensation is awarded, however, it will be deducted from any damages subsequently awarded in civil proceedings.

If criminal proceedings are being brought, this provision provides an easy and cost-free method by which a tenant can obtain compensation. However, amounts awarded by the magistrates' court under this provision tend to be less than the civil courts would award and therefore might not prove adequate compensation for the loss suffered. Furthermore, the criminal courts are not empowered to order a landlord to restore a dispossessed tenant to a property.

Civil proceedings

As has been shown above, criminal sanctions are often an inadequate remedy for a dispossessed or threatened occupier. The occupier may well need an injunction to restrain the landlord or to regain possession of the property. Damages and injunctions are only available in civil proceedings in the county court and often provide a more effective and speedy remedy; if need be, emergency procedures can be followed in order to obtain immediate relief (see pages 129–34). It is a popular fallacy that the law is incapable of moving swiftly in an emergency situation.

Causes of action

In order to bring civil proceedings in court a 'cause of action' is necessary. This means that the landlord must be shown to have broken some rule of law by his actions *and* to have caused the tenant to suffer loss or harm because of this.

Various causes of action are available to dispossessed or harassed tenants, some statutory and some based upon the common law, depending upon the facts of the particular case. It is advisable for the tenant to allege as many causes of action as is reasonably possible. Actions based both on contract law (i.e. the tenancy agreement) and the law of torts (civil wrongdoing) may be possible.

Actions for breach of contract
(1) Breach of the covenant for quiet enjoyment
It is an implied term of every tenancy that the landlord will allow his tenant 'quiet enjoyment' of the premises. Quiet is used here in the sense of 'peace', not absence of noise. Unlawful eviction and most actions of harassment will be a breach of this covenant.

(2) Breach of contract in general
Any other breach of a term of the tenancy or licence agreement will be actionable by the occupier. So if a landlord evicts a tenant before the end of the tenancy, e.g. before giving notice to quit, he will be in breach of contract. Similarly, if the landlord agrees to provide gas and electricity to a house and then withdraws these facilities, he will again be in breach.

Actions in tort
(1) Trespass to land
A tenant has the right to exclusive possession of the premises which have been let to him. If the landlord (or anyone else) enters those premises without permission he is liable for trespass. Licensees who do not have the right to exclusive possession cannot sue in trespass.

(2) Trespass to the person
Harassment and unlawful eviction are frequently accompanied by violence or threats of violence. These may well amount to the torts of assault and battery (which can also be criminal offences). Battery is the infliction of physical violence on another without lawful excuse; assault is any act which puts a person in immediate and reasonable fear of battery. This cause of action will be available to both tenants and licensees.

(3) Trespass to goods
If, in the process of harassing or evicting an occupier, a landlord damages the occupier's furniture or other personal belongings, this would amount to trespass to goods, i.e. unlawfully damaging someone else's property. If the landlord detains or otherwise deprives the occupier of the use of the goods, this might amount to a special tort called 'conversion'. Both tenants and licensees can use this cause of action.

(4) Section 3: Protection from Eviction Act 1977
Section 3 of the Act provides that when a tenancy or licence which is not 'statutorily protected' comes to an end, but the former tenant continues to reside on the premises, he cannot be evicted without a court order. Any evictions of such a tenant will give rise to an action in tort for breach of statutory duty.

The definition of a statutorily protected tenancy excludes assured and assured shorthold tenancies under the Housing Act 1988 and protected tenancies under the Rent Act 1977. Tenancies and licences will also be excluded if:

- the occupier shares accommodation with the landlord or licensor who occupies the premises of which the shared accommodation forms part as his only or principal home

125

- the occupier shares accommodation with a member of the landlord's or licensor's family who occupies the premises of which the shared accommodation forms part as his only or principal home
- they confer the right to occupy for the purpose of a holiday
- they were granted other than for money or money's worth (i.e. assets with a monetary value such as stocks and shares).

(5) Breach of Section 27 of the Housing Act 1988
Section 27 creates a statutory tort if a landlord:

- attempts unlawfully to deprive a residential occupier of his occupation and the occupier leaves as a result; or
- knowing or having reasonable cause to believe that his conduct is likely to cause a residential occupier to give up his occupancy, commits acts likely to interfere with the peace or comfort of the residential occupier or members of his household and the occupier leaves as a result.

Note that this tort is satisfied only if the residential occupier actually gives up occupancy; this cause of action cannot be used in cases of harassment which have forced the occupier to leave. Equally, there will be no liability under Section 27 if the occupier is reinstated in the property either by the landlord or by an order of the court.

The landlord has a defence to this action if he can prove that he had reasonable cause to believe that the occupier had ceased to live in the premises, or that he had reasonable grounds for his conduct. There is a special measure of damages for this tort (see below).

Remedies in civil proceedings

Damages

The basic remedy for breach of contract or tort will be damages, or compensation for loss. The measure of damages, i.e. the amount that can be recovered, will vary depending upon the cause of action alleged.

Measure for Section 27 actions

For actions under Section 27 of the Housing Act 1988 (see above) a special measure of damages is laid down (in Section 28). Normally damages are assessed on the basis of the loss to the plaintiff; under Section 28 the damages are assessed on the basis of the gain to the landlord, in an attempt to prevent landlords from profiting from their wrongdoing.

The damages awarded will be the difference between the value of the premises with a sitting tenant and the value with vacant possession. This difference in value could be quite substantial (over £30,000 in one actual case) and both plaintiff and defendant must be prepared to provide valuation evidence where a claim under Section 27 is being brought. The amount of the damages payable may be reduced by the court if the prior conduct of the tenant was such that it would be reasonable to reduce the damages or the tenant has unreasonably refused an offer of reinstatement.

With regard to the above points, it is not unknown for tenants to harass and assault landlords and so a reasonable reduction of damages might be available to a landlord who had decided to take the law into his own hands by way of retaliation. If the tenant has suffered a series of unpleasant events, it would not be considered unreasonable for him to refuse reinstatement when, in his mind at least, he might be placing himself at further risk.

Measure in other actions

Under the normal laws of tort, damages are designed to put the plaintiff in the position he would have been in had the tort *not* been committed. In contract law, on the other hand, damages are designed to put the plaintiff into the position he would have been in *had* the contract been fulfilled.

Obviously, in bringing a claim, full details of all losses suffered because of the landlord's actions should be kept. These will include the cost of any alternative accommodation that was necessary, the cost of damage to furniture, clothes, etc. Some losses, such as physical injury or mental stress suffered, are difficult to quantify and will only be quantified by the court if the case is successful.

127

Exemplary damages

Exemplary damages are available only for actions in tort, and will be awarded only where the defendant's conduct has been calculated to make a profit over and above any damages he would have otherwise had to pay to the plaintiff. They are available in unlawful eviction cases to teach wrongdoers that tort does not pay. It is not necessary to show that the landlord actually made a profit in order to claim exemplary damages, nor are they limited to the amount of profit actually made. They must, however, be specifically asked for in the particulars of claim. Although not available in contract actions, the special measure of damages under Section 27 of the Housing Act 1988 has a similar objective (see page 127).

Aggravated damages

Aggravated damages are also available only in relation to actions in tort, but unlike exemplary damages they need not be specifically claimed by the plaintiff. They are similar in many respects to exemplary damages, the difference being that there is no need to show an element of calculation on the defendant's part. They are primarily awarded in cases of particularly unpleasant conduct by the landlord.

Injunctions

Awarding damages in harassment and unlawful eviction cases will not necessarily provide the occupier with a full solution to his problem. An occupier who has been awarded damages but remains in occupation will want protection and reassurance that the harassment will not be repeated; an occupier who has been unlawfully evicted may want to be reinstated in the property; an occupier who has been deprived of his personal belongings will want them restored to him. The appropriate remedy in such cases will be an injunction. If an occupier fears that he may suffer unlawful eviction in the future he may also seek an injunction to restrain the landlord from such conduct. Unlike damages, however, an injunction is a *discretionary* remedy, which means that even if the tenant's case is proved the court does not have to grant an injunction; it will only do so if it thinks damages are an inadequate remedy. Furthermore, an applicant who delays bringing his case to court may fail to obtain an injunction, as may an applicant who has himself been guilty of violence against the landlord. However, neither of these circumstances would prevent a claim for damages.

An injunction may be made by the court as a final order or as an interim order. A final order is made on the final determination of the case, which may well be several months after the commencement of the proceedings. Obviously, in harassment cases such a delay will be unacceptable and so an interlocutory or interim injunction should be applied for. This will remain in force until a specified date, but will not necessarily reflect the final outcome of the case.

Interlocutory relief is not available as of right; various conditions must be satisfied. However, in harassment cases this should not cause any problem.

The requirements which must be satisfied are:

- that there is a serious case to be tried; and
- that damages would not be adequate compensation; and
- it is more convenient to grant an injunction rather to await the outcome of the full trial.

The applicant will usually be required to give an undertaking to compensate the landlord if it is later found that the order should not have been made. Even if the applicant is on legal aid (and therefore unable to give a financially worthwhile undertaking) this should not prevent the making of an interlocutory order in appropriate cases.

Normally an injunction is ordered by the court only after both sides to the action have been heard. However, in an emergency, an *ex parte* order can be obtained, i.e. an order made on the hearing of evidence from the applicant only. This kind of injunction is sought in many harassment and unlawful eviction cases where the occupier requires a speedy remedy.

Obtaining emergency relief

It is possible to bring proceedings for harassment or unlawful eviction on a 'self-help' basis, but it should be borne in mind that speed and accuracy are of the utmost importance if effective relief is to be obtained. As far as possible, therefore, professional help should be sought.

If you are eligible for legal aid, then a solicitor can be instructed at little or no cost. If not, assistance may be obtained from law centres, housing advice centres and Citizens Advice Bureaux. The local office of the county court (at which the proceedings have to be commenced) will also be helpful in providing the correct forms and ensuring that they have been properly completed, but it must be appreciated that the county court staff are not able to conduct cases in person on behalf of litigants.

Information needed to bring a court action

Whether you are instructing a solicitor or bringing the proceedings yourself, you will need to equip yourself with a large amount of information in order to commence the court proceedings.

The information should include:

(1) The precise identity of the property, including the postal address.

(2) The tenancy agreement and the rent book (if applicable). In a case of unlawful eviction it may well not be possible to obtain these owing to the fact that they are kept in the property from which the tenant has been evicted.

(3) The landlord's full name and address. It is important that some indication can be given to the process-server as to the landlord's likely whereabouts. The full names and addresses of anyone else involved in the harassment or eviction should also be obtained if at all possible.

(4) Full and precise details of the alleged harassment or the circumstances of the unlawful eviction. If there are any potential witnesses to the alleged acts, their names and addresses should be obtained. The clearer the details are of what has happened, the better the chance of obtaining effective relief.

Application on notice or *ex parte*?

Normally, notice of the proceedings should be served upon the landlord at least two days prior to the hearing of the application (on notice), but in an emergency an *ex parte* application may be made, i.e. an order made on the hearing of evidence from the applicant only. Most courts prefer the application to be made on notice if at all possible. If an *ex parte* order is made, it will only be valid for a short time until a further hearing (on notice) can be held.

Contacting the landlord

Whether or not an application is to be made *ex parte* or on notice, consideration should be given at the outset as to whether or not the tenant (or his solicitor) should contact the landlord. This course of action may well be ruled out due to the urgency of the situation. However, if at least telephone contact can be made, this may be helpful for a variety of reasons. It is usually preferable to settle the matter out of court if at all possible, and it may be that the landlord does not realise he is doing anything unlawful. In any event, a full record should be kept of any contact with the landlord, as when an injunction application is made it may be helpful to include details of the contact in a supporting affidavit (sworn statement) as further evidence of the landlord's conduct.

Commencing the proceedings

The procedure from this point onwards is described in detail below. Those who have a solicitor acting for them need not, of course, take direct responsibility for much of this, but will still benefit from knowing the process.

The proceedings should be commenced in the county court (address in the telephone directory). The court will be either the one for the area in which the premises are situated or the one for the area in which the landlord resides. Sometimes the tenant will have a choice of venue.

The next step, for cases where an *ex parte* application is to be made, is to warn the court (by telephone or letter) that such an application is intended and to ascertain when and where a judge will be available to hear the application. This can sometimes be a problem in rural areas where a judge is not in attendance every day, or even every week.

The following must then be sent or taken in person to the court:

(1) Request for issue of summons (Form N203).
(2) Particulars of claim, plus copy for service.

The particulars of claim must specify:

- the cause of action
- the relief or remedy sought
- the material facts on which the tenant is relying.

(3) Notice of application for interlocutory injunction (Form N16A) plus copy for service.

The notice of application must:

- state the terms of the injunction applied for
- be supported by an affidavit (sworn statement) in which the grounds for making the application are set out.

(4) Affidavit(s) from tenants and any witnesses, plus copies for service.

The affidavit must set out the grounds for making the application, including full details of the alleged events. In addition, where the order is sought *ex parte*, the affidavit must also explain why this is necessary.

(5) The prescribed fee.
(6) Except in an emergency, it will also be necessary to prepare a draft of the order required for approval by the judge if the application is successful. This will be in Form N16.

Serving the documents

If the application for the injunction is to proceed on notice (as opposed to an urgent *ex parte* application), the landlord should be served with the documents at least two days before the hearing of the application.

The documents to be served are:

- the notice of application
- a sealed copy of the summons
- a sealed copy of the particulars of claim
- a sealed copy of the affidavit.

Personal service arranged by the tenant (i.e., not through the court) is essential to avoid delay. It makes sense to use a professional process-server who is skilled in serving court papers as speedily and as safely as possible. Note that service may not take place on a Sunday, on Good Friday or on Christmas Day except, in urgent cases, with the leave of the court. An affidavit of service will be required from the process-server (Form N215) as, if the landlord does not appear, the tenant cannot proceed with the case.

The court hearing

Unless otherwise directed, every application (except those made *ex parte*) shall be made in open court. The application will be made to a single judge sitting alone without a jury. Many judges, however, will hear applications in chambers. The tenant(s) and any witnesses should attend and be prepared to give oral evidence, even though the court will have received their sworn statements.

The tenant will outline his case and then bring evidence to support his allegations. The landlord will then present his defence. Often the judge will be prepared to accept an undertaking from the landlord as to his future conduct *without* making a formal order. However, the landlord would still be in contempt of court should he not comply with such an undertaking.

The court order

The form of the injunction order will be decided by the judge, but a draft must be provided by the tenant. The terms of the injunction should be the same as those set out in the particulars of claim and in the notice of application. Prescribed Form N16 should be used as the basis of the order. An injunction should always be endorsed with a penal notice, i.e. a warning that failure to comply with the order may result in imprisonment for contempt (a recourse which without such a warning would be unavoidable).

The order must be served personally on the defendant before it can be enforced. Even if the landlord's whereabouts are unknown and he cannot be formally served with the order, steps should be taken to inform him of it, e.g. by telephone or hand-delivered letter. If he cannot be found then the remedy may well be ineffective.

Enforcement of the order

The tenant may apply for the landlord's committal to prison for contempt if he fails to comply with the terms of the order, but only if the order contains a penal notice (see above).

If enforcement should be necessary, an application should be made for issue of a notice warning the landlord that he must attend court to show cause why he should not be committed. This should be in Form N78 and it should:

- identify the provisions of the injunction alleged to have been broken
- list the ways in which they have allegedly been broken
- be supported by an affidavit stating the grounds upon which the application is made.

County courts have power to order a term of imprisonment for contempt for a fixed term not exceeding two years. The court also has power to order a fine instead of committal and to suspend the operation of a committal order. Usually, the commencement of committal proceedings will be sufficient to persuade a recalcitrant landlord to comply with the order; actual committal is comparatively rare.

Unless the judge orders otherwise:

- a copy of the order shall be served on the defendant either before or at the same time as the execution of the warrant; or
- where the warrant has been signed by the judge, the order for the issue of the warrant may be served on the defendant at any time within 36 hours after the execution of the warrant.

Q *My landlord came to see me yesterday and said that if I did not leave my flat by the end of the week he would come round with his mates and throw me out on the street. Can he do this?*

A No. He can only legally obtain possession by means of a court order. You should seek legal advice immediately and obtain an injunction against the landlord to prevent him taking any action such as he has threatened. You do not need to wait until he has actually carried out his threats before going to court.

Q *My landlord wants me to leave my flat, even though I am an assured tenant and have security of tenure. He has now offered me £1,000 to leave by the end of the month. Is this legal?*

A Provided that your landlord is not making any threats against you about what will happen if you do not leave, this is lawful. But you do not have to accept his offer; you have security of tenure and can stay on until he can prove a ground for possession against you. If you do choose to accept his offer, you will have to leave; it is up to you to decide whether losing your home is worth £1,000.

Q *My landlord has forced me to leave my flat. He made my life a misery for months, by banging on the door in the middle of the night, turning off the electricity for days at a time, threatening me with violence and so on. I eventually found somewhere else to live and have moved out. I don't want to go back there, but I don't want him to get away with it. What can I do? I am working so am not eligible for legal aid.*

A It certainly seems that you have the right to bring proceedings against the landlord under Section 27 of the Housing Act 1988 and possibly to obtain substantial damages. As you are aware, however, you would have to finance these proceedings yourself. Another possibility is to contact your local tenancy relations officer and see whether he would be willing to bring criminal proceedings against your landlord for harassment. The court could also award you compensation in criminal proceedings, although the amount would probably not be as large as under Section 27 proceedings.

CHAPTER 10

POSSESSION PROCEEDINGS

THIS CHAPTER describes the legal procedures which need to be followed if a landlord wants to bring possession proceedings against a tenant. Although the procedures vary depending on the type of tenancy, the following serves as a simplified guide to obtaining a court order for possession:

- the landlord serves a 'termination notice' on the tenant
- the landlord starts possession proceedings in the county court when the notice has expired
- the landlord provides evidence to prove his case
- an order is granted by the court.

These points are now considered in detail below.

Obtaining a court order for possession

As a general rule, a landlord must obtain a court order for possession if the tenant will not leave the landlord's property voluntarily. There are, however, some exceptions to the rule, known as excluded licences and tenancies. Where these apply, the landlord will *not* need a court order for possession, provided that he does not use or threaten violence towards the occupier. In cases where a physical confrontation between landlord and tenant is likely, the landlord is advised to obtain a court order anyway, as any violence may constitute an offence under the Criminal Law Act 1977.

A court order is not necessary if any of the following apply:

(1) Before the tenancy/licence was granted, the landlord/licensor occupied the property as his only or main home and, under the terms of the tenancy or licence, the occupier now shares accommodation with the landlord/licensor.

(2) The occupier shares accommodation with a member or members of the landlord's family and the following conditions are also fulfilled:

- the landlord/licensor's main home is in the same building (except a purpose-built block of flats)
- a member of the landlord's family shares accommodation with the tenant/licensee. (Family is widely defined to include husbands, wives, children, grandparents, grandchildren, brothers, sisters, uncles, aunts, nephews and nieces.)

(3) The occupier has failed to vacate a property let for the purposes of a holiday.

(4) The accommodation is available rent-free to the tenant.

(5) A tenancy or licence was given to a squatter or trespasser as a temporary measure.

(6) The accommodation is in a residential hostel.

However, in all cases other than those mentioned above, a court order is essential for landlords who wish to obtain possession of properties governed by either protected and statutory tenancies under the Rent Act 1977, assured and assured shorthold tenancies under the Housing Act 1988 or, in the public sector, secure tenancies under the Housing Act 1985. The procedure for obtaining a possession order varies according to the type of tenancy, although in each case the landlord will need to serve an appropriate *notice* on the tenant before starting legal proceedings. It is *vitally important that the correct notice is given*, as subsequent court proceedings may be invalid if the notice is defective. The different types of notice are described below.

Notice to assured shorthold tenants

Before starting possession proceedings the landlord must serve a termination notice under Section 21 of the Housing Act 1988.

This is known as the Section 21 notice, and it must be served *at least two months* before possession is required. The notice must be in writing but it does not have to be in a set form (although forms may be purchased from law stationers). A typical notice might be as follows:

Housing Act 1988

Section 21

Assured shorthold tenancy notice requiring possession

To: [name of tenant]

of: [address of tenant]

From: [name of landlord]

of: [address of landlord]

I/We hereby give you notice that I/We require possession of the dwellinghouse known as [tenant's address]

on: [date of expiry of notice] by virtue of Section 21 of the Housing Act 1988

Dated: [date of signature]

Signed: [landlord's signature]

(The name, address and dated signature of the landlord's agent should also be added, if applicable.)

Note that the two-month notice period is a *minimum* period; it can be longer. If an assured shorthold tenancy is granted for a fixed term of six months and the landlord intends to recover possession at the end of the term, he could give the Section 21 notice to the tenant at the beginning of the tenancy, stating that he will require possession at the end of the fixed term. A notice period of six months, as in this case, is perfectly valid. Notice can be served at any point during the fixed term, provided that it does not take effect *before* the fixed term expires. If the tenant does *not* move out at the end of the fixed term the landlord may start possession proceedings immediately without having to serve any further notices.

If the landlord does not serve the notice during the fixed term, but waits until the expiry of the tenancy, a different rule will apply, i.e. the termination date specified in the notice must be the *last* day of a rent period *at least two months* after the notice is given to the tenant. For example, an assured shorthold tenancy expired on 15 January 1994; no Section 21 notice was given before that date. The rent is payable monthly on the 15th of each month, which means the rental period runs from the 15th of one month to the 14th of the next. Therefore, the Section 21 notice should be given on or before 15 February 1994 to expire on 14 April 1994. This is the *minimum* notice period required; it could be longer.

It is very important to remember that rental periods can vary. If the rent was payable on a quarterly basis (rather than on a monthly basis as in the example above), the Section 21 notice would not expire for at least three months, on the last day of a rental quarter.

Notice to assured tenants

In order to start possession proceedings against an assured tenant, the landlord will need a court order based on one or more of the grounds for possession set out in Chapter 2. However, he must first serve a notice under Section 8 of the Housing Act 1988 (the Section 8 notice). This must be in the prescribed form (available from any law stationer). The notice must be served *at least two weeks* before any proceedings can be started in court but if Grounds 1, 2, 5, 6, 7, 9 or 16 (see Chapter 2) are used, *at least two months'* notice must be given. In the case of periodic tenancies, the notice cannot take effect any earlier than would a notice to quit. This means that if the rent under a periodic tenancy is payable quarterly, the Section 8 notice must allow at least three months before possession proceedings are commenced.

Notice to protected tenants under the Rent Act 1977

Protected tenancies are private tenancies granted prior to 15 January 1989 (see Chapter 4). In order to regain possession the landlord must serve a valid notice to quit, which again must be in a prescribed form, as available from any law stationer. If the tenancy is a periodic tenancy (e.g. weekly or monthly) the notice period must be a minimum of four weeks and the notice must contain certain prescribed information about the tenant's rights.

Although the law requires a *minimum* of four weeks' notice to quit, the actual notice period will depend largely on how the rent is paid. If, for instance, the rent is payable on the 15th of the month, at least one calendar month's notice prior to the end of a rental period (i.e. the 14th of the subsequent month) must be given. If the rent is payable quarterly at least three months' notice is required, to expire at the end of a relevant quarterly period.

In addition to giving the notice, the landlord will also need to prove one or more of the grounds for possession set out in the Rent Act 1977 (see Chapter 4).

Notice to statutory tenants under the Rent Act 1977

When a protected tenancy expires or is terminated by a notice to quit, the protected tenant becomes a statutory tenant and has the right to continue to live in the property on the same terms as before. A statutory tenancy is not strictly a tenancy in law but the Rent Act 1977 does give the statutory tenant a *personal* right to remain in occupation until the landlord obtains a court order under the Act. The landlord is not legally obliged to give notice to quit to terminate a statutory tenancy before commencing proceedings, but he would be well advised to do so, since the tenant should be given reasonable notice of the landlord's intention to apply for a possession order against him.

Notice to secure tenants under the Housing Act 1985

If a local authority or other public-sector landlord wishes to start possession proceedings against a secure tenant, he must serve a prescribed notice of intention (available from any law stationer). The notice must set out the grounds for possession and must give at least four weeks' notice of commencement of proceedings. The actual notice period will again depend on when the rent is due: e.g. if it is payable quarterly then at least three months' notice is required. Once the notice has been given it remains valid for 12 months, during which time proceedings can be instituted.

Notice to occupiers without security of tenure

Some occupiers are not covered by the statutory provisions mentioned above (see pages 137–8). In these cases, common law simply requires the landlord to give the occupier 'reasonable notice'. Unfortunately, the law does not define what is meant by the term 'reasonable'; it depends on the circumstances of the case. However, four weeks' notice should allow the tenant sufficient time to vacate the property. If the contract includes a set period of notice then the landlord must comply with these terms. In the case of a fixed-term contract which has expired, no notice at all is required before proceedings can be instituted. Again, however, it is wise to give the tenant reasonable notice.

When the notice expires

If the tenant has already vacated the property by the expiry date of the notice, then court proceedings will obviously be unnecessary. If the tenant has *not* vacated the property voluntarily, then the landlord will need to start possession proceedings in court.

Starting court proceedings

The landlord will need to start court proceedings in the county court for the district in which the property is located. Full details of this procedure are given on pages 144–5 (*An ordinary possession action*). However, it is first worth considering an alternative procedure which does not involve a court hearing and which is also much quicker. This is described immediately below.

The accelerated possession procedure

Introduced on 1 November 1993, the accelerated possession procedure is designed to award possession to the landlord without the need for a court hearing, provided he has a *mandatory* ground for possession. However, this procedure may be used only in the circumstances outlined below:

(1) The tenancy is an assured shorthold and the following conditions are satisfied:

- the terms of the tenancy are set out in a written agreement
- the tenancy agreement was made on or after 15 January 1989 and the tenant did not live in the property before that date
- the assured shorthold notice was served on the tenant *before* the tenancy was created
- the fixed term (minimum six months) has expired
- the tenant is the original tenant (i.e. the tenancy has not been assigned to anyone else during the course of the tenancy)
- the termination notice under Section 21 (minimum two months) has been served and has expired.

(2) The tenancy is assured (although not an assured shorthold) where the landlord is relying upon mandatory Grounds 1, 3, 4 or 5 (see pages 24–8), and notice that these grounds could be used was given to the tenant *before* the start of the tenancy.

In both cases, the landlord's claim must be limited to possession; if he is also claiming rent arrears he must use the ordinary possession procedure.

Assuming that the landlord is eligible to use the accelerated possession procedure, the first thing he must do is to complete an application for possession (available from the county court or any law stationer). The form explains that possession is being sought against the tenant, and on what ground(s), and that there will not normally be a court hearing. It must be supported by an affidavit (sworn statement) which is printed on the reverse side of the application form. This must be sworn before either a solicitor or an officer of the court. A copy of the tenancy agreement and notices served on the tenant must be attached to the form. The court then serves these papers on the tenant, who is allowed 14 days in which to reply on the printed form of reply which accompanies the papers. If the tenant does not reply within 14 days the landlord may apply for a possession order. To do this, he simply needs to tear off the relevant part of the notice of proceedings requesting judgment, and send it to the court.

If the court is satisfied that the landlord has a valid claim for possession, it will make an order for possession and notify both parties. If the court is *not* satisfied that the landlord's claim is valid, it will fix a hearing date and both parties will be asked to attend court.

If the landlord obtains an order for possession, the court will order possession in his favour within 14 days from when judgment is entered. However, if this would cause exceptional hardship to the tenant, the possession order may be extended up to 42 days from the date of judgment. The onus of proving exceptional hardship lies with the tenant.

An ordinary possession action

If the accelerated possession procedure is not appropriate, then the first course of action for the landlord is to send or take the following to the court:

- a summons for possession of property with a copy for each tenant (Form N5)
- the particulars of claim for possession with a copy for each tenant
- the court fee.

The particulars of claim must be laid out in a prescribed form. The grounds for possession must be specified, and if the claim is based on rent arrears details of all payments missed or not paid on time; it is permissible to attach a schedule setting out the relevant details. Details of steps already taken to recover rent arrears (if any) and the tenant's financial circumstances (if known) should also be entered. If the landlord is relying upon a discretionary ground, e.g. rent arrears, and considers that his own financial or other circumstances are relevant to the case, the form includes space for him to give details.

Service of the summons
The court will normally serve the summons and the particulars of claim on the tenant. This is normally done by first-class post and the landlord will be notified of the date of service. The landlord will also receive a notice of issue of the summons which will contain a date for hearing.

The tenant's reply
The tenant has 14 days in which to reply to the summons on the form supplied to him. However, this time limit is not strictly enforced: the tenant may reply at any time prior to the hearing date or even turn up at the hearing itself to give evidence as to why possession should not be granted.

The hearing
The landlord should attend the hearing, which is usually held at the district judge's court. He will need to present the tenancy agreement and the relevant notices and give evidence to prove his claim to possession. The tenant is entitled to attend and make his own representations.

The possession order

A possession order may be either absolute or suspended, depending on the circumstances. Alternatively, the court may refuse to make a possession order and simply dismiss the landlord's application for possession, or it may order an adjournment with or without conditions. The different types of order are outlined below.

Absolute order for possession
This means that the tenant must leave the property on the date specified in the order. An absolute order will be appropriate where the landlord proves a mandatory ground for possession. For example, if the tenancy is an assured shorthold and the

landlord has served the appropriate notices, the court has no choice but to make an order for possession requiring the tenant to vacate 14 days after the date of the hearing. The only discretion the court has in this case is to postpone the date for giving of possession for up to 42 days, but only if the tenant will suffer exceptional hardship. The onus is on the tenant to prove this. At the end of the stated period the tenant must vacate. Twenty-eight days is the normal discretionary period allowed by the court in possession cases.

An absolute order for possession would also be appropriate in the case of an ordinary assured tenancy (not a shorthold) when the landlord has served the requisite notice, e.g. basing possession on Ground 1: owner-occupier (see page 24). In cases where the tenant has no statutory protection under the Rent Acts or the Housing Acts (e.g. where there is a resident landlord) the court again must make an absolute order for possession.

Suspended order for possession
If the landlord proves a discretionary ground, the court may make an order for possession but 'suspend' the operation of the order if certain conditions are satisfied. Suspended orders are frequently used in rent arrears cases. Very often the court will make an order for possession which provides that if the tenant pays the current rent plus a certain amount of arrears each week or month, the order will be suspended and the tenant cannot be evicted. However, if he breaches the terms of the order the landlord may apply again to the court for the order to be made absolute or for an immediate warrant for possession to be issued, depending on the circumstances.

Adjournment
In cases where the landlord is relying upon discretionary and not mandatory grounds for possession the court need not make an order for possession at all. It may simply adjourn the proceedings, either to a later date or indefinitely, subject to certain terms and conditions. An adjournment may be appropriate if the tenant's conduct does not constitute a serious breach of the tenancy agreement, such as in a case based on rent arrears.

The court could, in the first instance, adjourn the case on condition that the tenant pays the current rent plus a certain amount of arrears each week or month. This is rather like a suspended order for possession, the difference being that no order for possession has in fact been made, which means that the landlord would have to re-apply to the court for a possession order if the tenant did not adhere to the terms. On the second occasion the court may make either a suspended order for possession or an absolute order for possession depending on the seriousness of the case and the tenant's circumstances.

Order against the landlord

If the landlord fails to make out a claim for possession (e.g. he has failed to serve the appropriate notices or they are defective) the landlord's proceedings may be dismissed. If this happens, the tenant can apply for an order for costs against the landlord (see below). If the tenant has made a counterclaim against the landlord (e.g. for breach of the landlord's repairing obligations, see Chapter 11) and succeeds with his claim, an order for damages may be awarded against the landlord.

Enforcement of possession orders

If the landlord has obtained an absolute order for possession and the tenant fails to vacate by the date stated in the judgment, the landlord must apply to the court for a 'warrant for possession'. He cannot simply enforce the order himself; it must be done through the court bailiff. This warrant for possession is an instruction to the bailiff to evict the tenant. The bailiff will send notice to the tenant of the date and time when the order will be carried out. The tenant may apply for the warrant to be deferred, but this will be granted only in exceptional circumstances.

In certain circumstances a tenant facing eviction may be rehoused by the local authority. The local authority has certain obligations under Part 3 of the Housing Act 1985 to house people who are not intentionally homeless (see page 161).

Legal costs incurred in possession proceedings

Responsibility for the legal costs incurred in possession proceedings is always a matter for the court's discretion. If a possession order is made against the tenant, the tenant may be ordered to pay some or all of the landlord's legal costs in bringing the proceedings. On the other hand, if the landlord fails and the tenant has incurred legal costs there may be an order for costs against the landlord. The successful party at the hearing will normally make an application for costs as appropriate.

Q *I let my flat to a tenant under an assured shorthold tenancy which has now expired. The tenant shows no sign of leaving voluntarily. How can I obtain possession?*

A If you have not already done so, you should serve a notice on the tenant under Section 21 of the Housing Act 1988, allowing at least two months' notice before the date specified for possession, which must be the last day of a rental period. If you served the notice before the expiry of the tenancy, you must make sure that the notice period has expired before you start court proceedings.

Assuming that the tenant does not leave by the due date, you may start either an ordinary possession action (in which case there will be a court hearing which you must attend to prove your case), or an accelerated possession action which will not require a hearing. You may not use the accelerated procedure if you are also claiming rent arrears.

Q *I let my house under an assured tenancy on a monthly basis. The tenant has not paid any rent for three months. How can I get possession?*

A You must first serve a notice on the tenant in the prescribed form under Section 8 of the Housing Act 1988, specifying the grounds upon which you are claiming possession. In your case, these will be Grounds 8, 10 and 11. You must attach full details of the grounds and the rent arrears to the notice and then allow two weeks before you start court proceedings.

When the notice expires you must file a county court summons and particulars of claim form (both available from the county court).

If the tenant does not leave voluntarily you must attend court on the hearing date given and prove your case. You will have to provide details of the rent arrears and produce the tenancy agreement. If you prove only Grounds 10 or 11 (which are discretionary), you will have to satisfy the court that your request for possession is reasonable. Much will depend on whether or not the tenant opposes your application.

Q *I am a resident landlord letting a bedsitter in my home to a student. I am not happy with the tenant and want him to leave. Do I need a court order?*

A Strictly speaking, you don't need a court order as this is an excluded tenancy. However, the safest option is to start possession proceedings in the county court. You must first give your tenant 'reasonable notice' of the termination of the arrangement (four weeks, say, although the period is not laid down in law), and if he remains after that time you should start court proceedings immediately. As long as you can prove that you have been a resident landlord throughout the tenancy and that you followed the correct procedure to terminate the agreement, you have a right to possession. The court cannot exercise discretion in this matter.

CHAPTER 11

DEFENDING POSSESSION PROCEEDINGS

A TENANT who is faced with possession proceedings and the prospect of eviction should not despair. A possession order against him is by no means inevitable. He has the right to reply to the possession proceedings *and* to attend any hearing to give evidence and present his case. The following factors should also be taken into account:

- in most cases the landlord will need to obtain a court order for eviction; the only exceptions are certain excluded tenancies and licences (see pages 137–8)
- a court order cannot be made unless the landlord proves his case
- the tenant may have a valid defence to the landlord's possession proceedings and/or a possible counterclaim against the landlord
- even if the landlord does prove his case, in many situations the court may have some discretion over whether or not to order possession
- even if the landlord does obtain an order for possession the court may have some discretion as to the date when it takes effect.

In addition, if the tenant needs legal advice or representation he may qualify for legal aid.

Various legal aid schemes are available. If the tenant merely wishes to obtain legal advice and assistance he can ask to be advised under the 'green form scheme'. The solicitor will determine whether or not the client is eligible for this. If the tenant is on income support and his capital does not exceed the prescribed amount he will automatically qualify for green form assistance, which enables the solicitor to give preliminary advice and assistance but not to take steps in the proceedings themselves or to represent the tenant at the hearing.

If the solicitor is required to represent the tenant in the proceedings at court an application should be made for a civil legal aid certificate. Again, the solicitor will complete the necessary forms with the tenant. For a civil legal aid certificate to be granted the Legal Aid Board must be satisfied as to the tenant's financial situation and that there are reasonable grounds for the tenant defending the landlord's possession action or making a counterclaim against the landlord. If a civil legal aid certificate is granted the solicitor will be able to act for the tenant throughout the proceedings, including representation in court.

Even if the tenant has not applied for legal aid and is unrepresented on the day of the hearing, some courts operate a duty solicitor scheme, whereby a solicitor on standby may act for the tenant. In addition, 'assistance by way of representation' may be authorised by the court where there is a solicitor within the precincts of the court on the day of the hearing, provided that the tenant would otherwise be unrepresented, that a legal aid certificate is neither in existence nor has been refused, and that the court is satisfied that the hearing should proceed on that day.

A Citizens Advice Bureau or a housing advice centre may also be able to assist the tenant with possible courses of action when faced with possession proceedings.

Filing a defence or counterclaim

After the landlord has filed a possession summons or an application for possession the county court will serve this on the tenant by post. The tenant should receive the summons and the particulars of claim and, in the case of the accelerated possession procedure described on pages 143–4, a copy of the landlord's application and affidavit as well. The tenant will also receive a form for reply. This form is intended to establish whether the tenant has any defence or counterclaim against the landlord and will also disclose the tenant's financial and personal circumstances, which the court will need to take into account in exercising its discretion where appropriate. The forms should be properly completed by the tenant and returned within 14 days of receipt of the summons. However, this 14-day time limit is not strictly enforced. The form may be returned at any time before the hearing, but if its late return results in an unnecessary adjournment the tenant could be ordered to pay the costs of that adjournment.

In planning a defence or counterclaim the tenant should bear in mind the following questions:

- what is his position as regards security of tenure?
- has the landlord complied with all the necessary legal formalities in bringing the proceedings?
- is the landlord able to prove the necessary ground for possession?
- if the landlord is relying upon a discretionary ground, is it reasonable for the court to make an order for possession?
- if the landlord is relying upon a mandatory ground, is there any way in which this can be challenged?
- is the landlord in any way in breach of his obligations under the tenancy agreement which may form the basis for a counterclaim?

These matters are worth considering separately.

Security of tenure

The tenant will usually enjoy security of tenure to some degree. This will depend on what type of tenancy he has, as outlined below:

- if the tenancy was granted prior to 15 January 1989 and is covered by the provisions of the Rent Act 1977 (see Chapter 4), the tenant will have substantial security of tenure
- if the tenancy was granted on or after 15 January 1989 the provisions of the Housing Act 1988 will usually apply (see Chapter 2). Assured tenants will enjoy substantial security of tenure, but assured shorthold tenants will have very little protection

• if the tenancy is a secure tenancy under the Housing Act 1985 (see Chapter 6), the tenant will enjoy substantial security of tenure.

The tenant should always check that the landlord has correctly set out the statutory provisions that apply to the tenancy in the particulars of claim. If the landlord's case has been wrongly stated this error may form the basis of a defence. For example, the parties may have entered into what appears to be an assured shorthold tenancy under the Housing Act 1988 but which, on further investigation, turns out to be a protected tenancy under the provisions of the Rent Act 1977. If the landlord now seeks to obtain possession under the purported assured shorthold tenancy, the tenant would be entitled to put in a defence which would result in the dismissal of the landlord's claim.

Legal formalities

The tenant should check that the landlord has complied with all the necessary formalities required by law, both in relation to the creation and termination of the tenancy and to any notices that should have been given; e.g. if the landlord is relying upon the fact that the tenancy is an assured shorthold, a prescribed notice stating that the tenancy was to be an assured shorthold should have been given before the tenancy agreement was entered into. If this was not done or the notice was not in the correct form the tenancy would amount to an ordinary assured tenancy (with full security of tenure) and *not* an assured shorthold tenancy. If the landlord then institutes proceedings on the basis that the tenancy is a shorthold, the tenant will have a possible defence.

The landlord's termination notices should also be checked. If the tenancy is an assured shorthold the landlord should have served a valid notice under Section 21 of the Housing Act 1988 and this must have expired before the proceedings were commenced. If this was not done, or was done incorrectly, the tenant will again have a defence.

Similarly, in the case of an assured tenancy which is not a shorthold the landlord should have served a termination notice under Section 8 of the Housing Act, setting out his grounds for possession. These grounds must be the same grounds as those which appear in the landlord's particulars of claim. If this is not the case, this point should be raised by the tenant either in the reply form or at the hearing.

If the tenancy is a secure tenancy (see Chapter 6) the landlord should have served a prescribed notice of intention to seek possession under the Housing Act 1985. Again, the tenant should check that the relevant grounds for possession have been included.

Grounds for possession

The grounds for possession stated in the landlord's particulars of claim must be proved by the landlord if the case is to succeed. The landlord must bring the necessary evidence to prove that, on the balance of probabilities, the grounds exist. If the grounds are disputed the landlord's evidence may be challenged by the tenant, which may result in the dismissal of the possession action.

A further point to remember is that certain grounds are mandatory (i.e. the court must make a possession order if the ground is proved), while others are discretionary (i.e. a possession order may not be made even if the ground is proved). The tenant should always check the landlord's notice to see which grounds he is using.

Discretionary grounds

If the landlord is relying on a discretionary ground, then in addition to proving the ground, the court must also be satisfied that it is reasonable to make an order for possession. Any order made can be suspended or postponed if the court thinks it just or equitable to do so. The court also has the power to adjourn the proceedings (see pages 146–7). Each case will be considered on its own merits and clearly much will depend upon the nature of the ground and the seriousness of the tenant's breach or breaches of the tenancy agreement. The tenant can state mitigating or personal circumstances in his reply to the possession summons which could influence the court's decision. In addition, the tenant should attend court on the hearing date to give his version of events.

155

Mandatory grounds

If the landlord is relying upon a mandatory ground for possession the tenant's position is much weaker. If the landlord proves to the court's satisfaction that the mandatory ground exists the court *must* make an order for possession. Moreover, under Section 89 of the Housing Act 1980 the order for possession must take effect 14 days from judgment unless it appears to the court that exceptional hardship would thus be caused to the tenant. If this is the case the court may use its discretion to postpone the date for handover of possession for up to, but no longer than, six weeks after the making of the order.

It must be borne in mind that most mandatory grounds require the landlord to have served a notice on the tenant before the tenancy was created, although the court does have the power to dispense with the notice requirement if it considers it just and equitable to do so (not in the case of assured shorthold tenancies).

Obviously any prejudice to the tenant will be taken into account by the court; e.g. if the tenant did not know that a mandatory ground existed before the tenancy was created the court is most unlikely to exercise its discretion in the landlord's favour.

One mandatory ground that does not require a prior notice to have been given to the tenant is assured tenancy Ground 8: rent arrears (see page 29). Even in this case, however, the court must be satisfied that the rent is not only three months in arrears, but also that it was 'lawfully due' on the relevant dates. The words 'lawfully due' may present problems for the landlord since the rent is not lawfully due unless the landlord, either in the tenancy agreement or separately, has given the tenant a written notice under Section 48 of the Landlord and Tenant Act 1987 with an address within England and Wales for the service of notices. The rent is due only from the date when the notice is given, a point which could be relevant in determining whether or not three months' rent actually is outstanding on the date when the landlord commences proceedings.

Fixed-term tenancies

Some tenancies are for a fixed term, e.g. six or 12 months rather than periodic, e.g. from month to month or week to week. If this is the case and the fixed term has not yet expired, the landlord faces a further hurdle if he is claiming possession. Even if the landlord has a ground for possession he must also show that there is a clause in the tenancy agreement which allows the fixed term to be brought to an end *before* it expires. There will normally be a forfeiture clause in the agreement which allows the landlord to repossess the property if the rent is in arrears or if a tenant is in breach of his obligations. However, not all grounds for possession will entitle the landlord to invoke this forfeiture clause. In the case of a fixed-term or assured shorthold tenancy the landlord must show that the tenancy agreement makes *express* provision for termination on the relevant ground. Many of the grounds which do not include rent arrears or breach of obligation, e.g. Ground 1: owner-occupier (see page 24), will not be expressly provided for in the tenancy agreement and the forfeiture clause will not be wide enough to cover the landlord's application for possession. The landlord's application for possession during the fixed term will therefore fail. The tenant will need to check the terms of his agreement carefully before completing his reply to the possession summons.

Making a counterclaim

If the landlord is in breach of his obligations under the tenancy agreement, the tenant may have the basis for a counterclaim. For example, in many tenancy agreements the landlord is under an obligation to repair the structure and exterior of the property and the installations within for the supply of gas, water, electricity, heating and sanitation. If the landlord ignores these obligations the tenant may have a claim for damages against the landlord. In some cases it may even be possible to offset the damage against rent arrears.

It is important that the tenant fills in the form of reply correctly if he intends to pursue a counterclaim. He should set out details of the alleged breaches of the landlord's obligations and the losses which he has suffered as a result, e.g. cost of repairs or decoration, damages for ill-health resulting from the disrepair. These matters may be vital in a possession case based on rent arrears.

Q *I have an assured shorthold tenancy (six months) which expires next month. The landlord says he wants me to leave when it ends, but I have nowhere else to go. What are my rights?*

A The landlord may not evict you without a court order and he cannot obtain this during the six-month fixed term, so you cannot be forced to leave on the last day of the tenancy. In addition, if he has not already done so, the landlord must serve you a notice under Section 21 of the Housing Act 1988 giving you at least two months' notice to quit. He cannot start court action until the notice has expired.

You should also check that the landlord has created a proper assured shorthold tenancy. You should have received a notice to the effect that the tenancy was to be an assured shorthold before you signed the tenancy agreement, you should have been granted possession for at least six calendar months (i.e. not five months and 27 days), and there should be no clause in the agreement allowing the landlord grounds for possession (except for rent arrears or breaches of obligation). If you find that the tenancy is not a proper assured shorthold you should defend the possession proceedings.

Q *I have received a summons seeking possession of my house based on rent arrears. I get housing benefit but this does not cover the whole rent. Am I likely to be evicted?*

A This will depend on what type of tenancy you have and the amount of rent arrears. If you are a Rent Act tenant or a secure tenant, the chances of the court making an absolute possession order against you at the first hearing are slim. You should fill in the reply form received with the summons and explain your position at the hearing on the date stated. The most likely outcome is a suspended order for possession, which means you don't have to leave your house if you pay the amount specified.

Q *I have stopped paying rent because the landlord will not do any repairs to my flat. The flat is cold and damp and the plumbing needs mending. The landlord is now threatening me with court action. What is my position?*

A You may not withhold rent unless you have incurred expense for repairs for which the landlord is liable. If the tenancy is for a period of less than seven years, the landlord is probably liable for the repairs you have mentioned. You should give the landlord written notice of the need for repair and obtain estimates for the work. On serving the landlord with these estimates you should tell him you will get the work done if he refuses to do so, and that you intend to deduct the cost from the rent arrears.

CHAPTER 12

REHOUSING

LOCAL authorities in England and Wales have certain obligations to house the homeless. The relevant law is contained in Part 3 of the Housing Act 1985 although the original legislation goes back to 1977. The legislation is designed primarily to help people who are:

- homeless or threatened with homelessness
- in priority need
- not intentionally homeless.

The local authority has a duty to rehouse an applicant only if all the relevant criteria are satisfied. A person may well be in priority need for housing but if he is not yet homeless or threatened with homelessness the local authority has no legal obligation to provide accommodation. Similarly, a person may be homeless and in priority need but if he left his previous accommodation voluntarily the local authority does not have a duty to provide him with permanent accommodation. The meaning of these various terms is explained below.

Homeless or threatened with homelessness
A person is deemed to be homeless if he has no accommodation that he is legally entitled to occupy. He does not, of course, need to be the owner of that accommodation: he could be a tenant or a licensee and the basis of his right to occupy may be very tenuous. If court proceedings have been instituted against the occupier and an order for possession has been made against him, then he would be considered 'threatened with

homelessness'; however, if he is to be evicted within the next 28 days he will be considered homeless.

A person is also deemed homeless if he has accommodation but he cannot gain entry to it (e.g. he has been unlawfully evicted) or if it is probable that his occupancy will lead to violence from some other person (whether that person also lives there or not). Furthermore, if an applicant's existing accommodation is a mobile home, caravan, house-boat, etc., the applicant may be deemed homeless if there is no place where he is entitled to put it and live in it. In addition, a person housed in temporary accommodation (such as a women's refuge or a night shelter) may be considered homeless for the purposes of the Act.

In priority need

A person is in priority need if he/she:

- has dependent children residing with him or who might reasonably be expected to reside with him
- is homeless or threatened with homelessness as a result of an emergency (e.g. fire, flood, other disaster)
- (or anyone who resides with him or who might reasonably be expected to reside with him) is vulnerable by reason of old age, mental illness or handicap, physical disability or other reason
- is a pregnant woman or resides with or might reasonably be expected to reside with a pregnant woman.

The Department of the Environment has issued a code of guidance which deals with the question of priority need. Although the authorities are not bound to comply with the guide they must have regard to it in the discharge of their duties under the Act.

Not intentionally homeless

An applicant is deemed to be *intentionally* homeless if he commits some deliberate act or omission which makes him unable to occupy his existing accommodation, or if he leaves his existing accommodation without good reason. In these circumstances, the local authority will have no obligation to rehouse him. Although all this may sound perfectly reasonable, difficulties arise in practice; e.g. if the tenant has been served with a notice to quit and vacates the property only to discover later that the notice was invalid, would he be considered intentionally homeless? The courts will usually take the view that if a tenant leaves because of a genuine mistake or ignorance of his rights (as in this case), this does not constitute a deliberate act or omission.

The duty of the local authority

When an application for rehousing is made to the local authority, the authority is obliged to find suitable temporary accommodation for the applicant pending its enquiries into his claim. If the authority is then satisfied that the applicant satisfies all the above criteria, it has a duty to provide permanent housing. However, this will be subject to availability and the applicant may remain in temporary accommodation for some time.

The local authority to which an application is made will not necessarily be the authority that ultimately deals with the matter. The application may be referred to another local authority within whose area the applicant has associations, such as a job or family connections.

Q *I am a single person living alone in a one-bedroom flat rented from a private landlord. I have an assured shorthold tenancy which is about to expire and my landlord wants me to leave. I have just been made redundant and doubt that any other private landlord will grant me a tenancy. Can I apply to the local authority?*

A You are entitled to seek advice and assistance from your local authority and you may be granted temporary accommodation. You may also apply for permanent accommodation but will not automatically qualify since you are not 'in priority need'. However, you should qualify for housing benefit which can be paid direct to a landlord; this may help you to find a landlord willing to grant you a tenancy despite the fact you are unemployed.

Q *I have lived with my boyfriend for over two years in a one-bedroom flat which he rents privately. I am now pregnant and the flat will not be big enough for all of us when the baby arrives. Are we eligible to rent a bigger flat from the council?*

A You should apply immediately to the local authority for assistance; your case will be considered sympathetically as pregnancy is considered a 'priority need'. However, the local authority is under no obligation to rehouse you now as you are neither homeless nor threatened with homelessness within 28 days.

CHAPTER 13

LONG LEASES OF HOUSES: THE RIGHT TO BUY THE FREEHOLD OR AN EXTENDED LEASE

THE Leasehold Reform Act 1967 as amended in 1993 (see below), gives valuable rights to tenants of houses with long leases at a low rent (commonly called ground rent). Leases were often granted for terms of 99 years or longer where the tenant had either built the house at his own cost on land belonging to the landlord or had in effect purchased the house (i.e. paid the equivalent of the full purchase price for the house as a premium for the granting of the lease); but until 1967 there was no way in which the tenant could acquire the freehold of his property or demand any extension of the lease when it was about to expire.

The 1967 Act gave these tenants the right to buy the freehold (known as 'enfranchisement') or to extend the lease for a further 50 years. The Act was amended by the Leasehold Reform Housing and Urban Development Act 1993. For either of these rights to apply certain conditions must be fulfilled:

- the tenant must be an individual (i.e. not a limited company)
- the tenant must have a lease of a house
- the tenant must have occupied the house as his only or main residence for the whole of the last three years or for a total of three out of the last ten years
- the tenant must have a long lease
- the rent must be low
- in some cases the house must fall within certain rateable value limits.

These terms are now explained below.

Houses

A house is defined to include any building designed or adapted for living in provided it is reasonable to call it a house. Most detached, semi-detached and terrace houses will clearly fall within this definition but flats and maisonettes are excluded. The 1967 Leasehold Reform Act covers houses only; leasehold owners of flats and maisonettes have rights under the Leasehold Reform Housing and Urban Development Act 1993 (see Chapter 14). In the case of a mixed-user property, e.g. a house with a shop and a flat above, provided the entire building may reasonably be called a house and the tenant has a lease which includes both the house and the flat, the 1967 Act will apply.

However, problems may occur if a large house has been converted into flats. If a tenant has a lease for the whole house he may be entitled to acquire the freehold or an extended lease of the entire building, whereas a tenant of an individual flat does not have this right.

Three years' occupation

Although the tenant must have occupied the property as his only or main house for at least three years or for a total of three years out of the last ten, he need not have lived in the whole of the house (i.e. he could have sublet part of the house and occupied the remainder).

Long lease

A long lease is a lease granted for a term exceeding 21 years. However, a tenant will not be disqualified from buying the freehold or extending the lease if there are less than 21 years unexpired at the date of his application; the important point is that the lease was originally granted for more than 21 years. Furthermore, the tenant does not have to be the original tenant: he may be an assignee (i.e. someone who bought the lease at a later date).

Low rent

Originally, in order to qualify under the 1967 Act, the rent had to be less than two-thirds of the rateable value of the property (pre-poll tax and council tax). The amended rules are complex but, as a general rule, the important factor is the rent which was payable during the first year of the lease. If no rent was payable during the initial year it will automatically satisfy the 'low rent' condition. If, as is more likely, rent *was* payable during the initial year then the date of the lease must be taken into consideration. For leases entered into before 1 April 1963, the rent during the initial year must not exceed two-thirds of the letting value of the property (as assessed by a chartered surveyor or qualified valuer) on the date of the start of the tenancy. If the lease was entered into between 1 April 1963 and 1 April 1990 and the property had a rateable value at the date of the start of the tenancy then the rent during the initial year must not exceed two-thirds of that rateable value. For leases granted on or after 1 April 1990 the initial rent must not have exceeded £1,000 if the property is in Greater London or £250 elsewhere. Most leases that were granted at a ground rent will meet these low rent criteria.

Rateable value limits

Originally, certain high-value premises with a high rateable value were excluded from the 1967 Act. This was so that most ordinary houses would be within rateable value limits. These rateable value limits have now been removed for tenants wishing to buy the freehold, but for tenants wishing to extend their leases the limits remain. Rateable value limits depend upon the location of the house, the date upon which the tenancy was created and when the house first appeared on the rating valuation list. The rules are complex and tenants wishing to extend their lease should seek professional advice.

Freehold or extended lease?

The tenant who satisfies the above conditions will normally wish to purchase the freehold, i.e. enfranchise, as the acquisition of the freehold will greatly enhance the value of his property. If, however, the tenant elects to buy an extended lease instead, a new lease will be granted for the unexpired remainder of the existing term plus a further 50 years. This new lease will operate

167

on much the same terms as the existing lease and the rent will remain the same until the end of the original term.

At the start of the 50-year extension, however, the rent will be increased to current ground rent levels, to be reviewed again after 25 years. In the long term, therefore, extending the lease will cost more than buying the freehold.

Another advantage of buying the freehold is that the covenants and conditions contained in the lease will cease to be enforceable. This is not the case with an extended lease.

The 'desire notice'

When the tenant has decided whether he wishes to acquire the freehold or an extended lease, he must formalise his choice by serving upon the landlord a written notice of his desire (the 'desire notice') in the prescribed form (available from any law stationer). The desire notice is treated as a contract and the landlord must serve a notice in reply within two months admitting or objecting to the tenant's claim.

The price of the freehold

For valuation purposes it is assumed that the landlord is selling the freehold subject to the lease and that the lease has already been extended for a further 50 years under the Act; it is also assumed that the tenant is not the prospective purchaser and that the freehold is being bought largely for its investment income (i.e. the ground rent). The fact that the tenant can, on acquisition, merge the freehold and leasehold interests is usually ignored. For certain higher-value properties, however, this 'marriage value', as it is sometimes called, may be taken into consideration.

The help of an expert valuer will be needed if the parties cannot agree the price between themselves. The tenant also has the right to appeal to a leasehold valuation tribunal.

Q *I bought my house 20 years ago and have lived in it ever since. It has a 999-year lease dating from 1900, fixed at a ground rent of £5 per year. I am keen to buy the freehold. Can I force the freeholder to sell and how much is it likely to cost?*

A It is highly likely that you can force the freeholder to sell the freehold to you. The house has been your only residence for over three years, the rent is obviously low and the other conditions laid down by the Leasehold Reform Act seem to be satisfied. You should first ask the freeholder if he will sell to you voluntarily; £5 a year is unlikely to be an important asset to him unless the lease includes clauses (restrictive covenants) which he wants to retain. If the freeholder won't sell, a 'desire notice' claiming the freehold should be served on him. It is best to employ a solicitor to do this as the procedure can be complicated. The price is negotiable, but is usually assessed at between 10 and 20 times the ground rent. Therefore, the basic price should be between £50 and £100 unless there are exceptional factors. However, bear in mind that you will also have to pay the freeholder's legal and surveying fees as well as your own.

Q *I am thinking of buying a house which has only a 50-year lease, but am worried that I may have difficulty selling it in a few years' time. The house is subject to a ground rent of £25 per year and the current tenant has lived in the house for over three years. Will I be able to buy the freehold or an extension of the lease?*

A If you buy the house now you will have to live in the property for at least three years before you can force the freeholder to sell or grant you an extension of the lease for a further 50 years. Therefore, it might be worth negotiating with the *existing* tenant; if he serves a 'desire notice' either to buy the freehold or a 50-year extension he could include a clause in the contract to sell the house saying that the benefit of the desire notice will be assigned to you. In this way you would not have to wait three years before being able to assert your right to buy the freehold or an extension of the lease.

CHAPTER 14

LONG LEASES OF FLATS – ACQUIRING THE FREEHOLD OR AN EXTENSION

IN MOST cases, when someone buys a flat he does not buy the freehold, which would give him the right to occupy the property for ever; instead he acquires a long lease for a fixed number of years. However, many 'long' leases are only for 99 years, or even less, and when there are less than 50 years left to run it can prove difficult to find a buyer. Moreover, tenants often complain that landlords do not undertake necessary maintenance and repair work, or that they overcharge for it when they do. This problem is particularly common amongst tenants who live in blocks of purpose-built flats.

The Leasehold Reform, Housing and Urban Development Act of 1993 has now given flat-owners the right to join together and collectively buy the freehold in their block (e.g. mansion flats). This will enable them to take over the management of the block themselves and also to grant themselves new long leases when their existing leases become unsaleable. It must be emphasised from the outset that only the freehold in the *whole* block can be bought; it is not possible to acquire the freehold in an individual flat in such circumstances. In addition, the freehold can only be acquired jointly with the owners of the other flats in the block (see pages 172–3).

If a flat-owner cannot afford to buy the freehold (and this might be quite expensive), he also has the right to buy a new lease of his individual flat, which will add a further period of 90 years to the existing lease. For many people, particularly where the existing system of management for the block is working satisfactorily, this will be a better option than buying the

171

freehold. This right can be exercised whether or not the other flat-owners wish to do so.

Both the right to buy the freehold (or 'enfranchisement', as it is sometimes called), and the right to buy a new long lease can be exercised without the landlord's consent, although there are limited grounds on which the landlord can resist a claim to enfranchise (see page 175).

It is not necessary for all the flats in a particular block to be let exclusively to tenants on long leases or exclusively for residential purposes; it is still possible, for instance, to buy the freehold or an extended lease if some of the flats are let to Housing Act tenants or occupied for business purposes.

Qualifying conditions

Various conditions have to be fulfilled before a tenant is entitled either to buy the freehold or to extend the lease on his flat. The conditions are somewhat complex, since both the tenant *and* the block of flats must 'qualify' under the Act, and, in the case of enfranchisement, a minimum number of qualifying tenants in the block must join in the purchase: at least two-thirds must participate, and at least half of them must satisfy the 'residence qualification' (see below). The tenants can then exercise their right to enfranchise by serving the appropriate notice on the freehold owner.

The tenant qualification

In order to qualify to buy the freehold or extend the lease, the flat-owner must be the tenant of a flat under a long lease and at a low rent. These requirements are explained separately below.

The tenant

A tenancy is defined to include a sublease, so a tenant still has rights under the Act even if his immediate landlord does not himself own the freehold. However, a tenant will not qualify if he occupies the property for the purposes of a business or if his immediate landlord is a charitable housing trust and the flat forms part of the accommodation provided by it for its charitable work. A tenant will also be disqualified if he owns qualifying leases of more than two flats in the same building.

Long lease
The definition of a long lease is a lease that was originally granted for a term exceeding 21 years. An applicant will qualify whether or not he is the original tenant, and it does not matter if there are now less than 21 years of the lease left to run.

Low rent
Whether the lease is deemed to be at a low rent will depend upon when it was first granted. In all cases, any payments made in respect of services, repairs, maintenance or insurance, even though reserved as rent, are to be excluded.

If the lease was granted before 1 April 1963, the rent must not have exceeded two-thirds of the letting value of the flat at the start of the lease. If the lease was granted on or after 1 April 1963 but before 1 April 1990, or on or after 1 April 1990 if the contract was *signed* before that date, the rent must not have exceeded two-thirds of the rateable value of the flat at the start of the lease. If the flat had no rateable value on that date, then the date when it first acquired one will apply. For leases granted after 1 April 1990, the initial rent must not have exceeded £1,000 if the flat is in Greater London or £250 elsewhere.

The residence qualification

The residence qualification will differ depending on whether the flat-owner wants to buy the freehold or a new lease. However, in both cases, if the flat is jointly owned with someone else, only one owner needs to satisfy the residence rule.

If a flat-owner wants to buy the freehold, he must have occupied the flat as his only or principal home for the last 12 months or three out of the last ten years (not necessarily consecutively).

If this residence qualification is not satisfied it may still be possible for the owner to join in a purchase of the freehold, since only half the tenants seeking to enfranchise need to have satisfied this rule.

If, on the other hand, the owner wants to buy a new lease, he must have occupied the flat as his only or principal home for the last three years or for three out of the last ten years (again not necessarily consecutively).

The building qualification

Once a qualifying tenant has satisfied the residence test, he will have the right to a new lease. However, in order to acquire the freehold, the building in which the flat is situated must also satisfy the Act's definition of 'premises', as outlined below:

- the building must be self-contained or form a self-contained part of a building
- the freehold must be owned by just one person
- the building must contain two or more flats held by qualifying tenants
- the number of flats held by qualifying tenants must not be fewer than two-thirds of the total number of flats in the building.

A building is deemed to be self-contained if it is structurally detached, while *part* of a building can only be self-contained if there is a vertical division between it and the rest of the building and its structure is such that that part could be redeveloped independently of the remainder. In addition, the services provided for the occupiers (e.g. gas, water, etc.) should be independent of the services provided for the rest of the building. This could be relevant, for example, in the case of a block of flats divided into two or more wings with separate entrances.

Excluded buildings

Certain buildings are excluded from the right to buy the freehold or a new lease, even though they may seem to satisfy the conditions mentioned above.

The excluded buildings are as follows:

- buildings within the precincts of a cathedral, National Trust property or property owned by the Crown
- buildings where any parts occupied or intended to be occupied for non-residential purposes (e.g. as a shop or office) exceed

10 per cent of the internal floor area of the premises. (In making this calculation, any common parts of the building are to be ignored.)

- converted properties containing four flats or fewer where the owner of the freehold (or an adult member of his family) has lived in one of the flats as his only or principal home for 12 months or more.

Disputing the tenant's claim

A landlord can dispute the tenant's right to enfranchise or to buy a new lease only if he can establish that one or more of the qualifying conditions has not been complied with by the applicants, or he can show that he intends to redevelop the whole or a substantial part of the premises. This ground for opposition will only be possible where not fewer than two-thirds of the long leases in the block are due to terminate within five years and the landlord cannot reasonably carry out his redevelopment without obtaining possession. It is unlikely in practice that this will apply very often.

Buying the freehold

The collective purchase of a freehold by qualifying tenants will cover not only the freehold of the premises in which the flats are situated, but also certain other property owned by the same freeholder. This will include any garage, car-parking space, outhouse, garden or yard, even if previously leased separately. In addition, if a subtenant has been granted a lease the head-lease must be acquired as well.

However, although the tenants will be buying the freehold, they are legally obliged to 'lease-back' parts of the building back to the freeholder on a 999-year lease at a peppercorn rent. This means, in effect, that no rent is payable for the leased-back property.

The following must be leased back to the original freeholder:

- flats let by the freeholder on secure tenancies
- flats let by housing associations on tenancies other than secure tenancies.

The following are to be leased back if the freeholder so requires:

- units which are not flats let to qualifying tenants. These could include unlet flats, or any part of the premises let on a business tenancy or on a tenancy which does include a long lease at a low rent
- a flat occupied by a resident landlord.

The first steps

The first thing to ascertain is that a sufficient number of other flat-owners are interested in acquiring the freehold. If at least two-thirds of the qualifying tenants are interested, the next step is to seek the advice of a valuer as to the likely price. If this is acceptable, then the purchase should be initiated by serving the appropriate notice on the freeholder. Again, professional advice will be necessary. Note that once this initial notice has been served, you can still change your mind and withdraw from the purchase, but you will have to pay the landlord's costs and expenses (as well as your own) if you choose to do so.

Nominating the new owner

All the tenants interested in buying the freehold should decide at an early stage who will buy the block on their behalf.

In the case of a small block, it may be advisable for the flat-owners to buy the freehold jointly and then hold it upon trust for themselves. However, no more than four people can be joint owners of one building, so in many cases it will be necessary to set up a limited company to buy the freehold, thus making the flat-owners shareholders in the company.

The price of the freehold or a long lease

Whether buying a new lease or the freehold in the whole block, the tenant will be paying the open-market price. In the case of a purchase of the freehold the tenant will pay the open-market price for the freehold and for any head-leases (see above) included in the acquisition. Each will be valued separately. It is essential to seek the advice of a qualified valuer or surveyor at an early stage to gain some idea of how much the freehold is going to cost. Note that compensation will have to be paid to the landlord if buying of the freehold reduces the value of other property in the locality belonging to him. The landlord's reasonable costs and his share of the 'marriage value' (see below) will also have to be paid.

Marriage value

Marriage value is a complex valuation principle based on the idea that when both the freehold and leasehold interests in a block are owned by the same people (as they will be after enfranchisement), the interests will be worth more together than when they were owned by different people. This is because the flat-owners can now grant themselves new leases on much more favourable terms than they might have got from a stranger. As the value of a block of flats generally increases when both the leasehold and freehold interests belong to the same person, the landlord is entitled to at least 50 per cent of this marriage value which, in some blocks of flats, could be a substantial amount.

Q *I have a long lease with 50 years left to run in a block of 25 flats. Should I buy my freehold?*

A Although you cannot acquire the freehold in your own particular flat, you have the right to get together with your neighbours and buy the freehold in the whole block. This would normally mean setting up a limited company to buy the freehold on behalf of all of you.

Building societies and banks are increasingly reluctant to lend on leases of less than 60 years. Buying the freehold would solve this problem, although it must be remembered that the procedure is very complicated and may be expensive. Assuming that the management of the block is acceptable, you should also consider the cheaper option of buying a new long lease.

CHAPTER 15

IN SCOTLAND: PRIVATE SECTOR TENANCIES

THE ACTS of Parliament which cover the law of landlord and tenant in Scotland are different from those which apply in England and Wales. Prior to 1989, this area of the law was covered by various Rent Acts, aimed at protecting tenants from exploitation and excessive rent demands caused by the scarcity of housing supplies. Although some types of tenancy enjoyed security of tenure and rent protection, many landlords tried to avoid the restrictions of the Acts.

Since the beginning of 1989, new private sector tenancies have been covered by the Housing (Scotland) Act 1988. This Act signalled a different approach to tenancies: private sector tenancies no longer have any protection as far as rent levels are concerned and tenants enjoy less security of tenure.

There are four essential elements in the creation of a tenancy under Scottish law:

- an agreement between the landlord and tenant
- the payment of rent. If someone is allowed to occupy a property rent free, this will not amount to a lease
- a fixed termination date (called an 'ish')
- possession.

The agreement must be in writing if the lease is for a year or more; leases of less than a year can be oral, although it is usually in the best interests of both parties to commit the lease to writing in case of future disputes.

It has been argued that the definition of a lease in Scotland covers contracts which are known as licences in England. The concept of a licence, to cover situations where there is no clear intention to create a landlord and tenant relationship (see pages 67–8), has not developed in Scotland and is not generally accepted.

Controlled tenancies

These existed prior to 1965 and were amalgamated into the protected tenancy sector in 1980, under the Tenant's Rights Etc. (Scotland) Act.

Protected tenancies

Before 1989, most private sector tenancies were likely to be protected tenancies. A protected tenancy is a contractual tenancy covered by the Rent (Scotland) Act 1984 and must satisfy the following requirements:

- the house must be let as a dwellinghouse (this can apply to a house or part of a house)
- the house must be a separate dwelling
- the rateable value must be less than a specified sum.

Various categories of tenancies, such as student and holiday lettings, did not qualify as protected tenancies.

A protected tenancy retains its status until the death of the tenant or his spouse, or any eligible successor, and therefore some protected tenancies are still in existence today.

Grounds for possession

As is the case in England and Wales, where there is a protected tenancy the landlord may repossess a property only by obtaining a court order. The landlord must first serve a notice to quit, giving a minimum of 28 days' notice. He must then show a ground for possession, either discretionary, where the sheriff *may* terminate the tenancy, or mandatory, where the sheriff *must* terminate the tenancy.

Discretionary grounds

Where a sheriff has discretionary grounds for repossession, he must not only be satisfied that the ground exists, but also that it is reasonable to grant an order for possession. The discretionary grounds for possession are similar to the grounds applied in England and Wales (see pages 53–7), and are as follows:

(1) Rent arrears or breach of the tenancy obligations.

(2) Nuisance, annoyance or using the house for immoral or illegal purposes.

(3) Deterioration of the condition of the dwellinghouse.

(4) Deterioration of the condition of furniture.

(5) Withdrawal of notice to quit by the tenant.

(6) Assignation or subletting of the whole house.

(7) House reasonably required by the landlord for occupation by a full-time employee.

(8) House reasonably required by the landlord for occupation as a residence for himself or a close family member.

(9) Excessive rent charged for a sublet.

(10) The house is overcrowded.

The last ground applies to situations where the house is so overcrowded as to be dangerous or injurious to the health of the inhabitants and the tenant has failed to take reasonable steps to alleviate the situation by the removal of any lodger or subtenant. In England and Wales, this is a mandatory ground for possession.

Mandatory grounds

If a landlord can establish one of the mandatory reasons for possession and the house is sought for the stated purpose, then the question of 'reasonableness' is not relevant and a sheriff *must* make an order for possession.

The mandatory grounds for possession are:

(1) The owner/occupier requires the house as his residence.

(2) The house is required as the owner's retirement home.

(3) The letting is an off-season holiday letting.

(4) The letting is to an educational body (but not students).

(5)   The letting is on a short tenancy.

(6)   The house is held for occupation by a minister or lay missionary.

(7–9)   The house is required for various agricultural purposes.

(10)   The house is designed and adapted for occupation by a person with special needs and is required for such a person. (There is no equivalent ground in the legislation for England and Wales.)

(11)   The landlord is a member of the Armed Forces and requires the house as his residence.

Fair rent system

A fair rent system similar to the system in England and Wales also exists for protected tenancies in Scotland. An application for a fair rent can be made by either the landlord or the tenant or by joint application to a rent officer (appointed by the Secretary of State for Scotland). After examining the property, the rent officer will determine a fair rent, using a pre-determined formula and taking into account various factors such as the area in which the property is situated.

If either the landlord or the tenant is unhappy with the rent officer's decision, the decision can be referred to a rent assessment committee, which may confirm, reduce or increase the rent. Both rent officers and rent assessment committees have a duty to have regard to all the circumstances (other than personal) of each case; in particular, they must apply their 'knowledge and experience of current rents of comparable property in the area'. This is different from the situation in England and Wales, where the test is of a market rent, which assumes there is no scarcity of accommodation (see page 60).

Once fixed, fair rents are valid for the next three years and the landlord is entitled only to the registered rent. However, a fresh application may be made within three years if there have been substantial changes in circumstances which result in the registered rent no longer being a fair rent.

Succession to protected tenancies

The Rent (Scotland) Act 1984 provides that certain members of the tenant's family may succeed to the tenancy. The right to succeed is restricted and certain criteria must be satisfied. The order of succession which applies where a tenant dies on or after 2 July 1990 is as follows:

- **Death of a tenant** The tenant's surviving spouse or cohabitee succeeds where the house was that person's only or principal home at the time of the tenant's death. If there is no surviving spouse then a member of the tenant's family who was residing with the tenant at the time of death and for two years beforehand also has a right to succeed.
- **Second succession** Where the first successor was a surviving spouse and that spouse dies, there may be a further succession by a person who was a member of the *original* tenant's *and* of the surviving spouse's family, provided he had been residing with the first successor at the time of that person's death and for two years immediately prior to the first successor's death.

If there are rival claims in either of the above cases, the question of succession will be decided by a sheriff.

Statutory tenancies

A statutory tenancy is one which arises when a tenant remains in possession of a house at the end of a protected tenancy, although he is not entitled to do so. The tenant can be evicted only if the landlord succeeds in obtaining a court order for repossession.

Assured tenancies

Under the Housing (Scotland) Act 1988, a new type of tenancy, known as an assured tenancy, was introduced to Scotland and became operational on 2 January 1989. This is essentially a tenancy at a market rent, with a reduced degree of security of tenure. Significantly, the 1988 Act abolished any method of regulating the rent which a landlord may charge other than by the operation of market forces, i.e. the supply of property and the demand for it. This was part of the Government's plan to revitalise the independent rented sector in Scotland.

An assured tenancy has four elements:

(1) **The tenancy of a house** For a tenancy to exist, there must be an agreement, rent payable, a termination date and possession, as in all leases in Scotland.

(2) **The house must be let as a separate dwelling** A tenancy may be of a flat, part of a house, or even a single room, provided it is possible for the tenant to carry on the 'major activities of residential life' there, i.e. sleeping, cooking and feeding. A common scenario would be where the lease provides for the exclusive possession of one room with a shared kitchen and bathroom.

(3) **The tenant must be an individual** Where there are several tenants, at least one must be an individual; a company cannot be granted an assured tenancy.

(4) The tenant must occupy the house as his **only or principal home**.

Excluded tenancies

The following cannot be assured tenancies:

- tenancies entered into before 2 January 1989
- tenancies at a low rent (£6 from 2 January 1989)
- tenancies of shops or licensed premises
- tenancies of agricultural land or agricultural holdings
- lettings to students
- holiday lettings
- tenancies where the landlord is resident
- crown tenancies
- public sector tenancies
- shared ownership agreements
- protected tenancies, housing association tenancies and secure tenancies
- temporary accommodation for the homeless.

Market rent

The Government scheme to revive the private rented housing sector allows market forces to operate and rents to be fixed in the market by what landlords are able to charge willing tenants.

Therefore, assured tenants, unlike protected tenants (see page 181), do not have the right to apply for a fair rent adjudication.

When a negotiated rent period comes to an end and the landlord wants to increase the rent, he must serve a formal notice on the tenant. For a tenancy of six months or more, the minimum notice is six months; for a tenancy of *less* than six months, the required notice period is the length of the tenancy or one month, whichever is the longer.

There are three ways for a tenant to prevent a proposed rent increase from going ahead:

- the tenant can refer the notice to a rent assessment committee, before the date on which the new rent is to take effect (see below)
- the landlord and tenant can agree to a change in rent which is different from the change proposed in the notice
- the landlord and tenant may agree that there should be no change in the rent.

A new rent cannot take effect any earlier than one year from the date of the previous rent increase.

The rent assessment committee

Where a tenant refers a notice of increase to a rent assessment committee, the committee must consider what rent might reasonably be expected in the open market in a contractual tenancy granted by a willing landlord to a willing tenant. Relevant considerations include the capital value of the house and capital appreciation. In addition, the state of repair of the house and its age, character and locality are considered when deciding on a reasonable rent. Certain factors, such as any improvements by the tenant, will be disregarded.

Once the committee reaches a decision, the new rent is normally due from the date specified in the landlord's notice. However, if the committee feels that this would cause undue hardship to the tenant, it may postpone that date to a date of the committee's choosing.

In Scotland, landlords granting assured tenancies can avoid the rent assessment committee altogether by providing for a rent increase in the tenancy agreement, either by a specified sum or by a percentage of the rent. For instance, the specified sum could be related to some external measurement, such as changes in the Retail Price Index. There is no equivalent provision in English law.

Assignation and subletting

An assured tenant is not permitted to assign, sublet or part with possession of the property let to him without the landlord's consent. This applies to both the whole and any part of the house. The consent of the landlord *must* be obtained and cannot be presumed. The landlord can expressly prohibit assignation or subletting in the tenancy agreement, or alternatively, give his permission, with or without conditions.

The rights of subtenants are protected where a tenant loses his tenancy: a court possession order against a tenant will *not* apply to a subtenant. However, this protection applies only to subtenancies which are expressly approved by the landlord.

Tenancy agreements

A landlord must draw up a written tenancy agreement (or lease) for an assured tenant, stating the terms on which the tenant occupies the house, and provide the tenant with a copy, free of charge. If the landlord fails to do so, the sheriff may draw up such a lease or alter the document if it is inaccurate. Where the rent is payable weekly, the tenant must also be given a rent book in a specified form.

Succession on death

When an assured tenant dies, the surviving spouse can succeed to the tenancy, provided the house was his or her only or principal home.

This right does *not* apply where the deceased tenant was himself 'a successor', as is the case in the following circumstances:

- the tenant acquired the tenancy under the will or intestacy of a previous tenant
- the tenant succeeded to the tenancy under the terms of the Rent (Scotland) Act 1984
- the tenant was the sole survivor of a previous joint tenancy
- the tenant previously succeeded to a tenancy of the same or substantially the same property and remained there as a tenant.

Security of tenure

The general principle of security of tenure applies in assured tenancies. Under Scottish law, in the absence of a notice by either party, the contract will continue after the end of the contracted term. This is known as 'tacit relocation' and will continue automatically until one of the parties gives notice of termination. The tenant has a right to stay in the property and can only be made to leave by an order from the sheriff court. If the tenant refuses to leave the property, he will have 'a statutory assured tenancy'. In order to obtain a possession order from the court the landlord must follow the proper procedure, as outlined below.

Recovery of possession

As is the case with protected tenancies under the Rent (Scotland) Act 1984 and secure tenancies under the Housing (Scotland) Act 1987, a possession order will be given to end an assured tenancy only on specified grounds. It is also essential that the landlord must first have given the tenant notice that he intends to start possession proceedings, specifying the grounds relied on and giving minimum notice of between two weeks and two months. In Scotland, a notice is valid for six months and the landlord can start proceedings within that time.

Assuming that a proper notice has been served on the tenant, the landlord must then establish the grounds for the order. As in other types of tenancy, there are *mandatory* grounds, where the sheriff has no discretion and an order must be granted if the ground is established, and *discretionary* grounds, where the sheriff has discretion but must be satisfied that it is reasonable to grant the order.

Mandatory grounds

These are similar to the grounds under English legislation (see pages 24–9), and are available in the following circumstances:

(1) The landlord wants the property for his own home or it was formerly his own home.
(2) Repossession by lender following mortgage default.
(3) The property is being let as out-of-season holiday accommodation (but not for more than eight months).
(4) Student accommodation let out-of-term (where tenancy does not exceed 12 months).
(5) The property is required for occupation by a minister or full-time lay missionary.
(6) The landlord intends to demolish or reconstruct the property.
(7) The tenant dies.
(8) Rent arrears of more than three months.

Discretionary grounds

If these grounds are used, the landlord must also establish that it is reasonable for the sheriff to grant an order. This will include taking into account all the relevant circumstances affecting both parties, including their conduct, any possible hardship which might result if the order is granted, and the possibility of the tenant finding other accommodation. The grounds are similar to those under English law, and are as follows:

(1) Suitable alternative accommodation available (detailed criteria are laid down in the Act for this ground). This is a mandatory ground for possession under English law.
(2) Tenant withdraws his notice to quit and continues in possession.
(3) Persistent delay in payment of rent.
(4) Rent arrears at date of notice seeking possession and at date of starting proceedings.
(5) Obligations of tenancy broken or not performed.
(6) Deterioration of the condition of the property owing to waste, neglect or default.

(7) Nuisance or noise, or use of the property for immoral or illegal purposes.

(8) Deterioration of furniture.

(9) Tied accommodation, where employment of the tenant ends.

In addition to the need for notice of the landlord's intention to use certain grounds, the tenancy agreement itself *must* include specific provision for the termination of the tenancy if any of the following occur:

- mortgage repossession
- persistent delay in paying rent
- rent in arrears
- breach of the terms of the tenancy (other than rent)
- deterioration of the property or common parts
- nuisance or use of the property for illegal or immoral purposes
- deterioration of the condition of the furniture.

If a possession order is granted, it brings to an end the contractual rights of a tenant and those of any statutory assured tenant.

Short assured tenancies

The Housing (Scotland) Act 1988 also introduced 'short assured tenancies', a distinct form of assured tenancy for a minimum fixed term of six months. The landlord can regain possession, either automatically or on giving notice, or by using any of the mandatory or discretionary assured tenancy grounds noted above, provided that a prescribed notice has been served *stating* that the tenancy is a short assured tenancy. This notice must be served *before* the creation of the tenancy and indicates that the landlord will be able to evict the tenant provided that the proper notice (two months) is given. The notice must also inform the tenant that he has the right to apply to a rent assessment committee for a rent determination.

Determination of rent

If a tenant applies to have a rent decided by a rent assessment committee, the criterion the committee must apply is the current market rent; in reaching its decision, the committee will look at a number of comparable properties. It will not fix a rent unless the rent paid by the tenant, judged against rents charged locally, is *significantly higher* than the rent which the landlord might reasonably expect to be able to obtain. Any rent fixed by a rent assessment committee takes effect from a date set by the committee and the determination lasts for one year.

Recovering possession

A short assured tenant has no defence to a properly based possession action. The sheriff must grant an order for possession if he is satisfied that all of the following apply:

- the tenancy has reached its termination date
- no tacit relocation exists (see page 186)
- no further contractual tenancy is in existence
- the landlord has given notice to the tenant that he requires possession of the house.

The landlord must give at least two months' notice (or longer if this is provided for in the tenancy agreement). The notice can be served during the tenancy, or after the termination date. Any court proceedings for recovery of possession require the landlord to serve two forms of notice on the tenant:

- notice to quit
- notice of proceedings for possession.

Notice to quit
To be valid, a notice to quit must be in a prescribed written form and must be given not less than four weeks before the date on which it is to take effect (in some cases, 40 days' notice must be given).

189

Harassment and unlawful eviction

Scottish law contains similar provisions to English law (see Chapter 9) to prevent the harassment and illegal eviction of tenants.

'Unlawful eviction' exists where any person (not necessarily the landlord) unlawfully deprives the occupier of the house or any part of it, or attempts to do so. Such a person shall be guilty of an offence unless he can prove that he believed, and had reasonable cause to believe, that the tenant had ceased to reside on the premises.

The offence of harassment is committed if actions or omissions are done, with the intention of causing the tenant to:

- give up the occupation of the house or any part of it; or
- refrain from exercising any rights or pursuing any remedy to which he is entitled.

Harassment includes acts likely to interfere with the peace or comfort of the tenant or members of his household, and the persistent withholding of services reasonably required for the occupation of the house.

Chart 4: Private sector tenancies

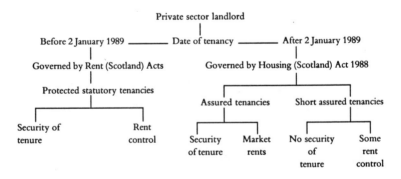

CHAPTER 16

IN SCOTLAND: PUBLIC SECTOR TENANCIES

IN SCOTLAND, a tenancy is a secure tenancy if:

● the house is let as a separate dwelling
● the tenant is an individual and the house is his only or principal home
● the landlord is one of a specified list of bodies, e.g. a district or regional council, Scottish Homes (see page 196), fire authorities.

However, there are various exclusions from secure tenancy status, as follows:

● premises occupied under a contract of employment for the better performance of duties
● a temporary letting to a person moving into an area to take up employment there and for the purpose of enabling him to secure accommodation in the area
● a temporary letting pending development affecting the property
● temporary accommodation during works on the property which the tenant normally occupies as his home
● tenancies granted to the homeless
● agricultural and business premises
● police and fire authority housing
● accommodation forming part of a building held for a non-housing purpose.

Tenancy agreements

All public sector tenants have the right to a written lease. It is the landlord's duty to draw up the necessary tenancy documents and to ensure that they are properly signed. The landlord must also give the tenant a free copy of the lease. Restrictions are placed on the landlord's powers to vary the terms of the lease without the tenant's consent; disputes between the landlord and tenant are resolved by the local sheriff court. If the landlord wishes to increase the rent, he must give at least four weeks' written notice of the increase.

Terminating a secure tenancy

There are five basic ways in which a secure tenancy can be terminated:

- agreement in writing between the landlord and tenant
- four weeks' notice by the tenant to the landlord
- the tenant abandons the tenancy
- no one is eligible or willing to succeed to a tenancy
- the landlord obtains a court order for recovery of possession.

Therefore, to regain possession of a house let under a secure tenancy where the tenant is unwilling to leave, a landlord must start court proceedings under the Housing (Scotland) Act 1987.

The procedure which must be followed includes:

- giving the tenant at least four weeks' notice of intention to take proceedings for recovery of possession (the notice must give details of the ground on which the landlord will rely in court)
- commencing court proceedings by serving a summons on the tenant within six months of the date specified in the notice.

The form of action is known as a 'summary cause' and is dealt with by the sheriff court for the area.

Grounds for possession

The Housing (Scotland) Act 1987 sets out certain criteria which must be satisfied before a sheriff will grant an order for recovery of possession. The landlord must establish either a mandatory or a discretionary ground for recovery of possession.

Discretionary grounds

In some cases, the sheriff has discretion to decide whether or not it is reasonable to grant an order. If he is not satisfied, the sheriff may refuse to make such an order. Discretionary grounds include:

(1) Non-payment of rent or breach of tenancy conditions.

(2) Conviction for using the property for immoral or illegal purposes.

(3) Waste, neglect and default leading to deterioration in the condition of the property.

(4) Deterioration of the condition of furniture due to ill-treatment by the tenant.

(5) Absence for a continuous period of six months or more/cessation of occupation as principal home.

(6) Grant of tenancy induced by a false statement.

(7) Nuisance or annoyance (serious anti-social conduct).

Mandatory grounds

If the landlord establishes a mandatory ground for recovering possession of a property, the sheriff has no discretion to refuse the order. However, the landlord must show that suitable alternative accommodation will be available to the tenant when the order takes effect. The mandatory grounds are:

(8) Nuisance or annoyance (less serious anti-social conduct).

(9) Overcrowding.

(10) Demolition or other substantial works.

(11) Premises designed or adapted for special needs.

(12) Houses designed or provided with, or located near, facilities for people with special social support needs.

(13) Housing Association providing housing for special categories of tenants (the old, infirm, disabled, etc.).

(14) The landlord's interest in house is that of a tenant and the lease has been terminated or will terminate within six months.

(15) The landlord is an Islands council and the house is held for education purposes and is required for those puposes, and the council cannot provide an alternative house, and the tenant is or was employed by the council in its functions as an Education Authority, and such employment is being terminated.

In cases where the landlord wishes to transfer the secure tenancy of a house to a tenant's spouse, former spouse or cohabitee, the sheriff must be satisfied both that it is reasonable to make an order *and* that suitable accommodation will be available to the tenant.

Succession on the death of a tenant

Under the Housing (Scotland) act 1987, there is a right of succession to a secure tenancy on the death of the tenant. This is limited to one succession only. Those entitled to succeed are:

- the tenant's spouse or cohabitee
- a surviving joint tenant
- where there is no one in either of the above two categories, a member of the tenant's family who is at least 16 years old and has lived in the house for at least 12 months prior to the tenant's death.
- if more than one person is entitled to succeed and the parties cannot agree amongst themselves who is to succeed, within four weeks of the tenant's death, the landlord can decide who succeeds.

Assignation, subletting and taking in lodgers

A public sector tenant has no right to assign, sublet, give up possession of a house or take in a lodger without first having his landlord's written consent. However, the landlord may not withhold his consent unreasonably. Subtenants do not have a secure tenancy nor do they have a protected tenancy or a statutory tenancy under the Rent (Scotland) Act 1984, or an assured tenancy under the Housing (Scotland) Act 1988.

The landlord can refuse to consent to subletting if the subtenant is not paying reasonable rent or has not paid a reasonable deposit as security for payment of bills or damage to the house or contents. If the landlord withholds consent, the tenant can apply to the sheriff for an order compelling the landlord to give consent. The sheriff will base his decision on relevant factors such as whether the consent would lead to overcrowding and whether the landlord proposes to carry out works on accommodation likely to be used by the subtenant.

Improvements

Provided a secure tenant has the landlord's written consent, he may carry out various alterations, improvements or additions to a house. The landlord must not withhold consent unreasonably. However, general repairs and maintenance do not need the landlord's permission, nor does interior decoration. The landlord may not increase the rent on the basis of the tenant's improvements; in some cases, it is possible for a tenant to obtain compensation for the cost of the works from the landlord at the end of the tenancy.

Repairs

Public sector landlords are obliged not only to carry out repairs to keep the house in a habitable condition, but also to keep in repair the structure and exterior of the house and to repair and keep essential facilities in proper working order (e.g. gas and electricity supplies).

Repairs after a tenant's application to buy
The landlord's responsibility for repairs ends when a tenant becomes the owner of a house. It is also important to be aware that there is a period between the lodging of an application to buy and the date of entry (when the house is paid for), when public sector landlords will accept responsibility only for minimal statutory repairs. This means the landlord will only carry out essential repairs, such as those needed to keep a house 'wind- and watertight' or relating to structural stability or health and safety matters. Even when a tenant becomes an owner, the title deeds for the house will usually include conditions concerning liability for repairs, including common repairs and maintenance charges for flats. Public sector landlords often provide a management (or 'factoring') service to deal with matters such as common repairs, grass-cutting, etc.

Scottish Homes

Scottish Homes is a government-funded housing agency which took over the responsibilities of the former Scottish Special Housing Association (SSHA) and the Housing Corporation in Scotland in 1989. The aim of Scottish Homes is to improve the choice and quality of housing available in Scotland, in partnership with both public and private sector landlords. The annual Scottish Homes budget is spent on a wide variety of activities including maintaining and improving Scottish houses, helping housing associations and co-operatives to provide more rented accommodation and giving grants to help people buy homes or to carry out environmental improvements. The agency also gives information and advice on a range of housing topics. There are 13 district offices in Scotland, with responsibility for the management of houses under Scottish Homes and providing services for Scottish Homes tenants. Scottish Homes headquarters are at Thistle House, Haymarket Terrace, Edinburgh EH12 5HE, tel. 031-313 0044.

Tenants' rights

Scottish Homes tenants have security of tenure and tenancy agreements which cover the following topics:

Rent
Scottish Homes has a 'rent fixing scheme' which is used to review rent each year. The scheme is used to reach an annual target or rental income from properties, taking various factors into account, including the value of houses, pre-set maximum and minimum rent increases, government subsidy and so on.

Succession
On death, the tenancy can be passed on to a husband or wife or to another family member over the age of 16, provided he has been living in the house for the previous 12 months. Only one succession to a tenancy is allowed.

Transfer
It is possible for tenancies to be transferred, either by agreement between the parties and Scottish Homes or following a court

order. With the consent of Scottish Homes, it is possible to arrange a mutual exchange. Other schemes, for exchange with tenants in other towns, are also in operation.

Tenancy agreements also deal with the question of lodgers, subletting, ending tenancies, repossession and other matters.

Tenant's choice

Under the Housing (Scotland) Act 1988, Scottish Homes is responsible for a 'tenant's choice' scheme which gives most public sector tenants the right to transfer to a landlord who has been approved by Scottish Homes, such as a housing association or a private landlord. An individual tenant may decide that he wishes to allow his house to be transferred. If so, the approved landlord requires the consent of the tenant and must then apply to acquire the house from the existing owner. The house is valued in accordance with a pre-determined formula, then the tenant is given a copy of the offer to sell (giving details of price and conditions) and has the right to negotiate and agree the terms of a new assured tenancy before the transfer of ownership is finalised. However, any new tenancies under this scheme will have less security of tenure than public sector tenancies.

Housing associations and co-operatives

Scottish Homes has the task of promoting and regulating housing associations and, since April 1989, has kept a register of these associations.

Housing associations are non-profit making, voluntary bodies, set up to build, improve and manage housing for people in need. All housing associations and co-operatives have a management committee, elected by the members, who are responsible for the running of the organisation.

There are various types of housing association and co-operatives, as outlined below.

Community-based housing associations
The 'community-based' designation is given to associations which:

- operate within a clearly defined neighbourhood
- have a substantial majority of their members living within the area
- are primarily concerned with the improvement of existing housing.

Tenant management co-operatives

A tenant management co-operative refers to a group of tenants who have collectively taken over some of the housing management functions for their houses, such as repairs and property management. These houses are owned by Scottish Homes, and members of the co-operative continue to pay rent, although there is an allowance from Scottish Homes to cover the maintenance responsibilities.

Par value co-operatives

These co-operatives undertake *full ownership*, control and responsibility for properties in their area. They are either fully mutual co-operatives, where all members are tenants, or non-fully mutual co-operatives where membership is not restricted to tenants.

Tenants' participation

Scottish Homes encourages the active involvement of tenants in decisions which affect their homes and neighbourhoods by promoting tenant participation in decisions on modernisation and improvement programmes, lettings, etc. In many cases, a group of tenants will form a tenants' association to share ideas for improvements and promote the interests of the people in their neighbourhood. These associations tackle a variety of issues, from environmental changes to refuse collection. Scottish Homes gives general advice and information to tenants' associations, including help in starting up and annual grants training.

The right to buy

Since 1980, secure tenants in Scotland have had the right to buy their homes. This right applies to both houses and flats. If the tenancy is with one of a specified list of landlords and the landlord owns the property concerned, the tenant may apply to buy, provided he has had a minimum of two years' continuous occupancy in public-sector accommodation. A tenant may be able to exercise his right to buy with other members of his family acting as joint purchasers. The right to buy does not apply to houses specifically designed for the elderly or the disabled.

The purchase price

The price for a house is fixed by subtracting a discount from the market value of the house. The landlord can choose whether the district valuer or a qualified valuer inspects and values the house. The valuation must not take account of any increase in value due to improvements carried out by the tenant.

The discount for houses starts at 32 per cent after two years' occupation and rises by 1 per cent for every following year, up to a maximum of 60 per cent. The discount for flats starts at 44 per cent and rises by 2 per cent for every following year, up to a maximum of 70 per cent. In the case of some newer houses, there may be a minimum price below which a house may not be sold.

The 1980 Act covers the sales procedure and conditions of sale and also the circumstances in which the landlord may refuse to sell.

Repayment of discount

If a house is resold within three years of the original purchase, the tenant will normally be required to repay some of the discount, as follows:

- 100 per cent of the discount if the house is sold within one year
- 66 per cent of the discount if the house is sold within two years
- 33 per cent of the discount if the house is sold within three years.

The right to buy on rent-to-mortgage terms

A rent-to-mortgage scheme was introduced in Scotland in October 1989, for a test period of three years. The scheme was initially administered by Scottish Homes but, with effect from 1 January 1994, all housing authorities (e.g. district councils) are required to offer the scheme. If a tenant wants to buy his home but has decided that the mortgage payments would be too high, a rent-to-mortgage scheme means that he can become the owner of his home by making mortgage payments which are no higher than the existing rent. The local authority or Scottish Homes gives the tenant a loan for the difference between the level of mortgage which the current rent payments would raise and the discounted purchase price. The loan does not have to be repaid until the house is sold or disposed of. The level of discount is less than under the right-to-buy scheme, ranging from 17 to 45 per cent for a house and 29 to 55 per cent for a flat. There are, however, various catergories of tenant who do not qualify for this scheme.

Chart 5: Public sector tenancies

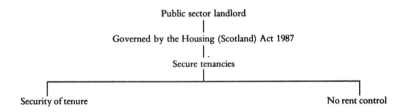

Practical tips for landlords and tenants

Letting mortgaged property
The mortgage lender should be consulted *before* tenants are sought to avoid delay when tenants are found. The lender may wish to approve both the tenants and the type of tenancy.

Letting leasehold property
Permission to sublet should be sought in advance. The lessor will probably require copies of prospective subtenants' references and of the proposed letting agreement.

Tenants' references
Landlords will normally require two referees for each tenant, one of them a character reference, the other from a bank or employer as evidence that the tenant is able to afford the rent. In the case of a company let a company search may be advisable.

Condition of property
Any landlord who wishes to let property should realise that it is in his own interests to put it into good decorative order, cleared of all personal effects that are not part of the inventory (see below) and thoroughly cleaned throughout. Paintwork should be in good condition, plumbing and wiring fault-free, and any electrical equipment supplied must be in good working order.

Inventories
It is in the interests of both parties to ensure that if property is being let furnished two copies of the inventory (updated by the landlord or his agent as necessary) are made available when the tenant moves in, one copy to be retained, the other to be signed and dated by the tenant, assuming he agrees that everything listed is indeed on the premises, and any defects noted, and returned to the landlord.

Contents of furnished property
The tenant may expect the property to contain all necessary furniture, major appliances (but not, usually, televisions and stereos), kitchen equipment and bedding (i.e. blankets, eiderdowns, pillows and duvets, but not, usually, linen).

Meter readings
Gas and electricity meters need to be read by landlord and tenant at the beginning and end of each tenancy and the relevant service provider notified. The accounts should be put in the name of the tenant. Tenants would be well advised to note the readings on the meters when moving into and out of a property.

Telephone bills
These, and reconnection charges, are the tenant's responsibility and the account is normally in the tenant's name. When vacating, the tenant should notify the telephone company in advance of the date when the telephone may be disconnected (unless otherwise arranged with the landlord) and the tenant's account closed.

Water rates
These are usually paid by the landlord.

Council tax
The tenant, under the Local Government Finance Act 1992, is obliged to pay this tax and to indemnify the landlord against any liability for this charge following the tenant's departure from the property at the end of the tenancy.

Insurance
It is the landlord's responsibility to insure the building and the contents he has himself provided, and to comply with the insurance companies' security requirements. The tenant may of course take out insurance to cover his own possessions, particularly any valuable items.

Keys
The landlord should provide a set of keys to the property for each occupant. These and any duplicates should be returned to the landlord at the end of the tenancy.

Viewing of property
It is usual for tenants to allow the landlord or his agents access to the property, by arrangement, during the last 28 days of a tenancy in order to show it to prospective new tenants.

Access to property
Unless an emergency arises, the landlord should not enter self-contained property lawfully let to a tenant without first obtaining the tenant's permission.

Forwarding address
The landlord is advised to obtain forwarding addresses for out-going tenants, especially if he has retained part of the deposit against expenditure/outstanding bills (see below). The tenant, even if he has made arrangements to have his mail forwarded by the Post Office, is advised to leave a forwarding address for any item that escapes this arrangement.

Deposits

On the termination of a tenancy, the landlord may retain part of the security deposit (which in total will usually have been the equivalent of four to six weeks' rental) to cover any outstanding bills expected and to rectify any damage and pay for any breakages. Cleaning of carpets, curtains, blankets, etc. may be charged to the tenant too if soiling is considerable.

Gardens

If the property has a garden, this should be tidy, with a mown lawn and pruned shrubs, at the start of the tenancy. It is in the landlord's own interest to provide basic garden tools, including a mower in good working order, so that the tenant can look after the garden during the tenancy.

Income tax

All income from rentals of property within the UK is liable to tax, wherever the landlord lives.

ASSURED TENANCIES: GROUNDS FOR POSSESSION

THIS IS the full, verbatim listing of the grounds for possession available under assured tenancies as laid out in Schedule 2 of the Housing Act 1988.

Mandatory grounds

Ground 1: owner-occupier
Not later than the beginning of the tenancy the landlord gave notice in writing to the tenant that possession might be recovered on this ground or the court is of the opinion that it is just and equitable to dispense with the requirement of notice, and (in either case):

(a) at some time before the beginning of the tenancy, the landlord who is seeking possession or, in the case of joint landlords seeking possession, at least one of them occupied the dwellinghouse as his only or principal home; or

(b) the landlord who is seeking possession or, in the case of joint landlords seeking possession, at least one of them requires the dwellinghouse as his or his spouse's only or principal home and neither the landlord (or, in the case of joint landlords, any one of them) nor any other person who, as landlord, derived title under the landlord who gave the notice mentioned above, acquired the reversion on the tenancy for money or money's worth.

Ground 2: mortgagee exercising power of sale
The dwellinghouse is subject to a mortgage granted before the beginning of the tenancy; and

(a) the mortgagee is entitled to exercise a power of sale conferred on him by the mortgage or by Section 101 of the Law of Property Act 1925; and

(b) the mortgagee requires possession of the dwellinghouse for the purpose of disposing of it with vacant possession in exercise of that power; and

(c) either notice was given as mentioned in Ground 1 above or the court is satisfied that it is just and equitable to dispense with the requirement of notice.

Ground 3: out-of-season holiday accommodation
The tenancy is a fixed-term tenancy for a term not exceeding eight months; and

(a) not later than the beginning of the tenancy the landlord gave notice in writing to the tenant that possession might be recovered on this ground; and

(b) at some time within the period of 12 months ending with the beginning of the tenancy, the dwellinghouse was occupied under a right to occupy it for a holiday.

Ground 4: out-of-term student accommodation
The tenancy is a fixed-term tenancy for a term not exceeding 12 months; and

(a) not later than the beginning of the tenancy the landlord gave notice in writing to the tenant that possession might be recovered on this ground; and

(b) at some time within the period of 12 months ending with the beginning of the tenancy, the dwellinghouse was let on a tenancy falling within paragraph 8 of Schedule 1 to this Act.

Ground 5: minister of religion's house
The dwellinghouse is held for the purpose of being available for occupation by a minister of religion as a residence from which to perform the duties of his office; and

(a) not later than the beginning of the tenancy the landlord gave notice in writing to the tenant that possession might be recovered on this ground; and

(b) the court is satisfied that the dwellinghouse is required for occupation by a minister of religion as such a residence.

Ground 6: demolition or reconstruction
The landlord who is seeking possession or, if that landlord is a registered housing association or charitable housing trust, a superior landlord, intends to demolish or reconstruct the whole or a substantial part of the dwellinghouse or to carry out substantial works on the dwellinghouse or any part thereof or any building of which it forms part, and the following conditions are fulfilled:

(a) the intended work cannot reasonably be carried out without the tenant giving up possession of the dwellinghouse because:

(i) the tenant is not willing to agree to such a variation of the terms of the tenancy as would give such access and other facilities as would permit the intended work to be carried out; or

(ii) the nature of the intended work is such that no such variation is practicable; or

(iii) the tenant is not willing to accept an assured tenancy of such part only of the dwellinghouse (in this sub-paragraph referred to as 'reduced part') as would leave in the possession of his landlord so much of the dwellinghouse as would be reasonable to enable the intended work to be carried out and, where appropriate, as would give such access and other facilities over the reduced part as would permit the intended work to be carried out; or

(iv) the nature of the intended work is such that such a tenancy is not practicable; and

(b) either the landlord seeking possession acquired his interest in the dwellinghouse before the grant of the tenancy or that interest was in existence at the time of that grant and neither that landlord (or, in the case of joint landlords, any of them) nor any other person who, alone or jointly with others, has acquired that interest since that time for money or money's worth.

(c) the assured tenancy on which the dwellinghouse is let did not come into being by virtue of any provision of Schedule 1 to the Rent Act 1977, as amended by Part 1 of Schedule 4 to this Act or, as the case may be, Section 4 of the Rent (Agriculture) Act 1976, as amended by Part II of that Schedule.

For the purposes of this ground, if, immediately before the grant of the tenancy, the tenant to whom it was granted or, if it was granted to joint tenants, any of them was the tenant or one of the joint tenants of the dwellinghouse concerned under an earlier assured tenancy or, as the case may be, under a tenancy to which Schedule 10 to the Local Government and Housing Act 1989 applied, any reference in paragraph (b) above to the grant of a tenancy is a reference to the grant of that earlier assured tenancy or, as the case may be, to the grant of the tenancy to which the said Schedule 10 applied.

For the purposes of this ground 'registered housing association' has the same meaning as in the Housing Associations Act 1985 and 'charitable housing trust' means a housing trust, within the meaning of that Act, which is a charity, within the meaning of the Charities Act 1960.

For the purposes of this ground, every acquisition under Part IV of this Act shall be taken to be an acquisition for money or money's worth; and in any case where:

(i) the tenancy (in this paragraph referred to as 'the current tenancy') was granted to a person (alone or jointly with others) who, immediately before it was granted, was a tenant under a tenancy of a different dwellinghouse (in this paragraph referred to as 'the earlier tenancy'), and

(ii) the landlord under the current tenancy is the person who, immediately before that tenancy was granted, was the landlord under the earlier tenancy, and

(iii) the condition in paragraph (b) above could not have been fulfilled with respect to the earlier tenancy by virtue of an acquisition under Part IV of this Act (including one taken to be such an acquisition by virtue of the previous operation of this paragraph), the acquisition of the landlord's interest under the current tenancy shall be taken to have been under the Part and the landlord shall be taken to have acquired that interest after the grant of the current tenancy.

Ground 7: death
The tenancy is a periodic tenancy (including a statutory periodic tenancy) which has devolved under the will or intestacy of the former tenant and the proceedings for the recovery of possession are begun not later than 12 months after the death of the former tenant or, if the court so directs, after the date on which, in the opinion of the court, the landlord or, in the case of joint landlords, any one of them became aware of the former tenant's death.

For the purposes of this ground, the acceptance by the landlord of rent from a new tenant after the death of the former tenant shall not be regarded as creating a new periodic tenancy, unless the landlord agrees in writing to a change (as compared with the tenancy before the death) in the amount of the rent, the period of the tenancy, the premises which are let or any other term of the tenancy.

Ground 8: substantial rent arrears
Both at the date of the service of the notice under Section 8 of this Act relating to the proceedings for possession and at the date of the hearing

(a) if rent is payable weekly or fortnightly, at least 13 weeks' rent is unpaid;

(b) if rent is payable monthly, at least 3 months' rent is unpaid;

(c) if rent is payable quarterly, at least one quarter's rent is more than 3 months in arrears; and

(d) if rent is payable yearly, at least 3 months' rent is more than 3 months in arrears;

and, for the purpose of this ground, 'rent' means rent lawfully due from the tenant.

Discretionary grounds

Ground 9: alternative accommodation
Suitable alternative accommodation is available for the tenant or will be available for him when the order for possession takes effect.

Ground 10: rent arrears
Some rent lawfully due from the tenant:

(a) is unpaid on the date on which the proceedings for possession are begun; and

(b) except where subsection (1)(b) of Section 8 of this Act applies, was in arrears at the date of the service of the notice under that section relating to those proceedings.

Ground 11: persistent delay
Whether or not any rent is in arrears on the date on which proceedings for possession are begun, the tenant has persistently delayed paying rent which has become lawfully due.

Ground 12: breach of covenant
Any obligation of the tenancy (other than one related to the payment of rent) has been broken or not performed.

Ground 13: waste or neglect
The condition of the dwellinghouse or any of the common parts has deteriorated owing to acts of waste by, or the neglect or default of, the tenant or any other person residing in the dwellinghouse and, in the case of an act of waste by, or the neglect or default of, a person lodging with the tenant or a subtenant of his, the tenant has not taken such steps as he ought reasonably to have taken for the removal of the lodger or subtenant.

Ground 14: nuisance
The tenant or any other person residing in the dwellinghouse has been guilty of conduct which is a nuisance or annoyance to adjoining occupiers, or has been convicted of using the

dwellinghouse or allowing the dwellinghouse to be used for immoral or illegal purposes.

Ground 15: damage to furniture
The condition of any furniture provided for use under the tenancy has, in the opinion of the court, deteriorated owing to ill-treatment by the tenant or any other person residing in the dwellinghouse and, in the case of ill-treatment by a person lodging with the tenant or by a subtenant of his, the tenant has not taken such steps as he ought reasonably to have taken for the removal of the lodger or subtenant.

Ground 16: former employee
The dwellinghouse was let to the tenant in consequence of his employment by the landlord seeking possession, or a previous landlord under the tenancy, and the tenant has ceased to be in that employment.

SAMPLE ASSURED SHORTHOLD TENANCY AGREEMENT

Note: do not use this agreement without studying the accompanying notes on pages 75–80.

THIS AGREEMENT is made on [insert date and year]

BETWEEN

(1) The Landlord [insert landlord's name].

(2) The Tenant [insert tenant's name].

IT IS AGREED as follows:

(1) The Landlord lets and the Tenant takes the premises being [insert name of property to let].

(2) The tenancy shall be for a term of [insert number of months/years] ('the Term') from and including [insert commencement date of tenancy] ('the Commencement Date').

(3) The Tenant shall pay to the Landlord the rent of £xx per [insert week/calendar month] (exclusive/inclusive of council tax and exclusive/inclusive of water charges) payable in advance on [insert day] of each [insert week/month] during the Term, the first such payment to be made on the signing of this Agreement for the period from the commencement date until the next rent payment date.

(4) This Agreement is intended to create an Assured Shorthold Tenancy as defined in Section 20 of the Housing Act 1988.

(5) The tenancy includes the Landlord's fixtures and fittings, furniture and effects as specified in the attached inventory ('the Fixtures and Fittings').

(6) 1. On the signing of this Agreement, the Tenant shall pay to the Landlord the sum of £xx [insert figure] ('the Deposit') by way of deposit as security for the Landlord in respect of the following:

   (a) any rent or any other monies which may be due to the Landlord but which remain unpaid
   (b) any damage to the Premises, or the Fixtures and Fittings or any other property belonging to the Landlord for which the Tenant may be liable
   (c) any unpaid accounts in respect of water, electricity, gas and telephone services provided to the Tenant by the Landlord or the respective suppliers
   (d) any other breach on the part of the Tenant of the Tenant's obligations under this Agreement.

2. The Landlord may at any time deduct from the Deposit any unpaid rent or other monies or any loss or expenses incurred or suffered by the Landlord or any sums expended by the Landlord arising out of the foregoing matters, but the Landlord shall notify the Tenant of any such deduction.

3. Provided that the Tenant has vacated the Premises and has returned all of the keys to the Premises to the Landlord, the Deposit shall be returned to the Tenant within one month following the expiration or determination of the tenancy. The Deposit will be returned after deducting all such rent and other sums referred to in subclause 1 above (if any), but in the event of them exceeding the amount of the Deposit then held by the Landlord, the amount of such excess shall be paid by the Tenant to the Landlord within 14 days of written demand.

4. If the Landlord sells or transfers his interest in the premises and pays the balance of the Deposit held by him (after deduction of all sums deductible under this Agreement) to the buyer or transferee, the Landlord shall be released from all further claims and liabilities in respect of the Deposit or any part of it.

5. The Deposit shall be paid into a separate interest bearing account with the [insert name of bank/building society] in the name of the Landlord and all interest earned shall be added to and held as part of the Deposit.

6. If at any time during the tenancy the amount then held by the Landlord as Deposit is less than the sum originally required to be paid by the Tenant, then the Landlord may require the Tenant to pay to the Landlord such amount as is required to increase the amount of the Deposit accordingly. The Tenant must pay this sum within 14 days of a written demand. In default of payment this amount may be recovered by the Landlord as rent.

(7) The Tenant agrees with the Landlord as follows:

1. (a) to pay the rent (and sums recoverable as rent) according to the terms of this agreement
   (b) in the event of any instalment of rent or any other money payable under this Agreement remaining unpaid after it has become due, then it will carry interest at the rate of 5 per cent per annum above the base rate of [insert name of bank] Bank plc from time to time in force from the date upon which the money became due until the date of payment.

2. To keep the interior of the Premises and the Fixtures and Fittings in good repair and condition throughout the Term (excepting only those installations which the Landlord is obliged to repair under Section 11 of the Landlord and Tenant Act 1985).

3. To make good (or, if required by the Landlord, to pay for) all damage to the Premises howsoever caused and to the Building caused by the act of omission of the Tenant or of any other person residing with or visiting the Tenant.

4. To make good or replace (or, if required by the Landlord, to pay for) all items of the Fixtures and Fittings which may, from whatever cause, be lost, stolen, broken, damaged or destroyed during the Term.

5. Upon not less than 2 days' notice (except in an emergency) to permit the Landlord and the Landlord's agents and any other persons authorised by the Landlord to enter the Premises (with or without workmen and with all necessary equipment) for any or all of the following purposes:

   (a) to examine the condition of the Premises or the Building or any adjoining or neighbouring property

   (b) to repair, maintain, alter, improve or rebuild the Premises or the Building or any adjoining or neighbouring property

   (c) to examine or to repair, maintain or replace the Fixtures and Fittings

   (d) to comply with any obligation imposed on the Landlord by law.

6. Not to do or omit to do anything:

   (a) which causes any policy of insurance on the Premises or the Building or the Fixtures and Fittings to be or to become void or voidable

   (b) which causes the rate of premium on any policy of insurance to be increased.

The Tenant will pay to the Landlord on demand all sums paid by the Landlord by way of increased premium and all other expenses incurred by the Landlord as a result of a breach of this provision.

7. Not to assign or sublet the Premises or any part of them.

8. Not to part with or share the possession of the Premises.

9. To permit the Premises to be viewed at any reasonable time by any person who is, or who is acting on behalf of, a prospective purchaser, prospective Tenant or prospective mortgagee of the Premises or of the Building.

10. Not to use the premises for any illegal or immoral purpose.

11. Not to do anything which may be or may tend to be a nuisance or annoyance or cause damage to the Landlord or to any neighbouring or adjoining property or to the owners or occupiers of any neighbouring or adjoining property.

12. To pay all charges in respect of any gas or electricity consumed on the Premises and in respect of any telephone installed on the Premises.

13. To pay the television licence fee for the Premises.

14. Not to keep any animals, birds or other livestock on the Premises.

15. To use the Premises for the purpose of a single private residence only.

16. Not to remove any of the Fixtures and Fittings from the Premises.

17. To notify the Landlord promptly in writing of any defect or disrepair in the Premises or the Fixtures and Fittings.

18. Not to make any alterations or additions to the Premises.

19. To pay to the Landlord all costs and expenses (including VAT) incurred by the Landlord (including, but not limited to, the costs and fees of the Landlord's solicitors and other professional advisors) in respect of:
    (a) the recovery from the Tenant of the rent or any other monies due from him; and
    (b) the enforcement of any of the provisions of this Agreement; and
    (c) the service of any notice relating to the breach by the Tenant of any of the Tenant's obligations under this Agreement.

20. To ensure that any garden enjoyed by the Premises is:
    (a) at all times during the Term kept in a neat and tidy condition; and
    (b) is properly cultivated; and
    (c) that any grass is cut at least once a week during the growing season.

21. To deliver up the Premises and the Fixtures and Fittings at the determination of the Term to the Landlord in a clean and tidy condition and in accordance with the Tenant's obligations under this Agreement.

(8) The Landlord agrees with the Tenant that the Tenant paying the rent and observing the obligations imposed on him in this Agreement shall peaceably hold and enjoy the Premises throughout the Term without any interruption by the Landlord or any person rightfully claiming through or in trust for him.

(9) IT IS AGREED as follows:

1. The Tenant shall not be entitled to withhold payment of any instalment of rent or any other monies payable under this Agreement on the ground that the Landlord has the deposit monies in his possession or on the ground that the Landlord is or may be in breach of any of his obligations to the Tenant whether under the terms of this Agreement or imposed by statute or otherwise.

2. This Agreement shall take effect subject to the provisions of Sections 11 to 16 of the Landlord and Tenant Act 1985 (as amended), which impose on the Landlord obligations as to the repair of the structure and exterior of the Premises and certain installations for the supply of water, gas, electricity and sanitation.

3. If the rent is inclusive of council tax and/or water rates, then in the event of there being any increase in the same, the Landlord may increase the rent by an equivalent amount.

4. The Landlord reserves the right to retain keys for the Premises.

5. If the Premises are rendered uninhabitable by fire or any other risk against which the Landlord may have insured, then the rent will cease to be payable until the Premises are reinstated. This provision will not apply, however, if the insurance monies are irrecoverable in whole or in part due to any act or omission on the part of the Tenant.

6. Where the expression 'the Tenant' comprises more than one person the obligations on the part of such persons shall be joint and several.

(10) 1. The Landlord/Tenant [delete as appropriate] shall pay the council tax in respect of the Premises.

2. The Landlord/Tenant [delete as appropriate] shall pay the water charges in respect of the Premises.

(11) The Landlord notifies the Tenant in accordance with Section 48 of the Landlord and Tenant Act 1987 that his address for service is [insert address for service].

(12) If at any time the rent (or any part) is unpaid for 14 days after becoming due (whether or not formally demanded) or if any agreement or obligation on the Tenant's part is not complied with, or if any of the circumstances mentioned in Grounds 8, 10, or 11 to 15 of Part II of Schedule 2 to the Housing Act 1988 shall arise, then the Landlord may re-enter the Premises and the tenancy shall be determined. This is to be without prejudice to any right of action the Landlord may have in respect of the Tenant's obligations under this Agreement. This right of re-entry is not to be exercised by the Landlord without a court order whilst anyone is residing in the Premises or whilst the tenancy is an assured tenancy.

IN WITNESS the parties have signed this Agreement as a deed on the date first mentioned.

Signed [landlord's signature] Landlord, in the presence of [witness' signature]

Signed [tenant's signature] Tenant, in the presence of [witness' signature]

SAMPLE ASSURED TENANCY AGREEMENT INCORPORATING A GROUND 1 NOTICE

Note: do not use this agreement without studying the accompanying notes on pages 75–80.

THIS AGREEMENT is made on [insert date and year]

BETWEEN

(1) The Landlord [insert landlord's name].

(2) The Tenant [insert tenant's name].

(3) The Guarantor [insert guarantor's name, if applicable].

IT IS AGREED as follows:

(1) The Landlord lets and the Tenant takes the Premises being [insert name of property to let].

(2) The tenancy shall be for a term of [insert number of months/years] (the 'Term') from and including [insert commencement date of tenancy] ('the Commencement Date').

(3) The Tenant shall pay to the Landlord the rent of £xx per [insert week/calendar month] (exclusive/inclusive of council tax and exclusive/inclusive of water charges) payable in advance on the [insert day] of each [insert week/month] during the Term, the first such payment to be made on the signing of this Agreement for the period from the commencement date until the next rent payment date.

(4) *Ground 1 notice*
The Landlord notifies the Tenant that possession of the Premises may be recovered under Ground 1 in Schedule 2 to the Housing Act 1988. This requires the court to order possession of the Premises where the Landlord has previously occupied the Premises as his/her only or principal home or requires the Premises as the only or principal home of the Landlord or the Landlord's spouse.

(5) *Ground 2 notice*
The Landlord notifies the Tenant that possession of the Premises may be recovered under Ground 2 in Schedule 2 to the Housing Act 1988. This requires the court to order possession where:

> (a) the Premises are subject to a mortgage or charge granted before the beginning of the tenancy; and
> (b) the Lender is entitled to exercise a power of sale; and
> (c) the Lender requires possession of the Premises in order to dispose of them with vacant possession when exercising the power of sale.

(6) The tenancy includes the Landlord's fixtures and fittings furniture and effects as specified in the attached inventory ('the Fixtures and Fittings').

(7) 1. On the signing of this Agreement, the Tenant shall pay to the Landlord the sum of £xx [insert figure] ('the Deposit') by way of deposit as security for the Landlord in respect of the following:

> (a) any rent or any other monies which may be due to the Landlord but which remain unpaid
> (b) any damage to the Premises, or the Fixtures and Fittings or any other property belonging to the Landlord for which the Tenant may be liable
> (c) any unpaid accounts in respect of water, electricity, gas and telephone services provided to the Tenant by the Landlord or the respective suppliers

(d) any other breach on the part of the Tenant and the Tenant's obligations under this Agreement.

2. The Landlord may at any time deduct from the Deposit any unpaid rent or other monies or any loss or expenses incurred or suffered by the Landlord or any sums expended by the Landlord arising out of the foregoing matters, but the Landlord shall notify the Tenant of any such deduction.

3. Provided that the Tenant has vacated the Premises and has returned all of the keys to the Premises to the Landlord, the Deposit shall be returned to the Tenant within one month following the expiration or determination of the tenancy. The Deposit will be returned after deducting all such rent and other sums referred to in sub-clause 1 above, (if any), but in the event of them exceeding the amount of the Deposit then held by the landlord, the amount of such excess shall be paid by the Tenant to the Landlord within 14 days of written demand.

4. If the Landlord sells or transfers his interest in the Premises and pays the balance of the Deposit held by him (after deduction of all sums deductible under this Agreement) to the buyer or transferee, the Landlord shall be released from all further claims and liabilities in respect of the Deposit or any part of it.

5. The Deposit shall be paid into a separate interest-bearing account with the [insert name of bank/building society] in the name of the Landlord and all interest earned shall be added to and held as part of the Deposit.

6. If at any time during the tenancy the amount then held by the Landlord as Deposit is less than the sum originally required to be paid by the Tenant, then the Landlord may require the Tenant to pay to the Landlord such amount as is required to increase the amount of the Deposit accordingly. The Tenant must pay this sum within 14 days of a written demand. In default of payment this amount may be recovered by the Landlord as rent.

(8) The Tenant agrees with the Landlord as follows:

1. (a) to pay the rent (and sums recoverable as rent) according to the terms of this Agreement

   (b) in the event of any instalment of rent or any other money payable under this Agreement remaining unpaid after it has become due, then it will carry interest at the rate of 5 per cent per annum above the base rate of [insert name of bank] Bank plc from time to time in force from the date upon which the money became due until the date of payment.

2. To keep the interior of the Premises and the Fixtures and Fittings in good repair and condition throughout the Term (excepting only those installations which the Landlord is obliged to repair under Section 11 of the Landlord and Tenant Act 1985).

3. To make good (or, if required by the Landlord, to pay for) all damage to the Premises however caused and to the Building caused by the act or omission of the Tenant or of any other person residing with or visiting the Tenant.

4. To make good or replace (or, if required by the Landlord, to pay for) all items of the Fixtures and Fittings which may, from whatever cause, be lost, stolen, broken, damaged or destroyed during the Term.

5. Upon not less than 2 days' notice (except in an emergency) to permit the Landlord and the Landlord's agents and any other persons authorised by the Landlord to enter the Premises (with or without workmen and with all necessary equipment) for any or all of the following purposes:

   (a) to examine the condition of the Premises or the Building on any adjoining or neighbouring property

   (b) to rep..r, maintain, alter, improve or rebuild the Premises or the Building or any adjoining or neighbouring property

   (c) to examine or to repair, maintain or replace the Fixtures and Fittings

   (d) to comply with any obligation imposed on the Landlord by law.

6. Not to do or omit to do anything:

    (a) which causes any policy of insurance on the Premises or the Building or the Fixtures and Fittings to be or to become void or voidable

    (b) which causes the rate of premium on any policy of insurance to be increased.

    The Tenant will pay to the Landlord on demand all sums paid by the Landlord by way of increased premium and all other expenses incurred by the Landlord as a result of a breach of this provision.

7. Not to assign or sublet the Premises or any part of them.

8. Not to part with or share the possession of the Premises.

9. To permit the Premises to be viewed at any reasonable time by any person who is, or who is acting on behalf of, a prospective purchaser, prospective Tenant or prospective mortgagee of the Premises or of the Building.

10. Not to use the Premises for any illegal or immoral purpose.

11. Not to do anything which may be or may tend to be a nuisance or annoyance or cause damage to the Landlord or to any neighbouring or adjoining property or to the owners or occupiers of any neighbouring or adjoining property.

12. To pay all charges in respect of any gas or electricity consumed on the Premises and in respect of any telephone installed on the Premises.

13. To pay the television licence fee for the Premises.

14. Not to keep any animals, birds or other livestock on the Premises.

15. To use the Premises for the purposes of a single private residence only.

16. Not to remove any of the Fixtures and Fittings from the Premises.

17. To notify the Landlord promptly in writing of any defect or disrepair in the Premises or the Fixtures and Fittings.

18. Not to make any alterations or additions to the Premises.

19. To pay to the Landlord all costs and expenses (including VAT) incurred by the Landlord (including, but not limited to, the costs and fees of the Landlord's solicitors and other professional advisors) in respect of:

    (a) the recovery from the Tenant of the rent or any other monies due from him; and

    (b) the enforcement of any of the provisions of this Agreement; and

    (c) the service of any notice relating to the breach by the Tenant of any of the Tenant's obligations under this Agreement.

20. To ensure that any garden enjoyed by the Premises is:

    (a) at all times during the Term kept in a neat and tidy condition; and

    (b) is properly cultivated; and

    (c) that any grass is cut at least once a week during the growing season.

21. To deliver up the Premises and the Fixtures and Fittings at the determination of the Term to the Landlord in a clean and tidy condition and in accordance with the Tenant's obligations under this Agreement.

(9) The Landlord agrees with the Tenant that the Tenant paying the rent and observing the obligations imposed on him in this Agreement shall peaceably hold and enjoy the Premises throughout the Term without any interruption by the Landlord or any other person rightfully claiming through or in trust for him.

(10) IT IS AGREED as follows:

1. The Tenant shall not be entitled to withhold payment of any instalment of rent or any other monies payable under this Agreement on the ground that the Landlord has the deposit monies in his possession or on the ground that the Landlord is or may be in breach of any of his obligations to the Tenant whether under the terms of this Agreement or imposed by statute or otherwise.

2. This Agreement shall take effect subject to the provisions of Sections 11 to 16 of the Landlord and Tenant Act 1985 (as amended), which impose on the Landlord obligations as to the repair of the structure and exterior of the Premises and certain installations for the supply of water, gas, electricity and sanitation.

3. If the rent is inclusive of council tax and/or water rates, then in the event of there being any increase in the same, the Landlord may increase the rent by an equivalent amount.

4. The Landlord reserves the right to retain keys for the Premises.

5. If the Premises are rendered uninhabitable by fire or any other risk against which the Landlord may have insured, then the rent will cease to be payable until the Premises are reinstated. The provision will not apply, however, if the insurance monies are irrecoverable in whole or in part due to any act or omission on the part of the Tenant.

6. Where the expression 'the Tenant' comprises more than one person the obligations on the part of such persons shall be joint and several.

(11) 1. The Landlord/Tenant [delete as appropriate] shall pay the council tax in respect of the Premises.

2. The Landlord/Tenant [delete as appropriate] shall pay the water charges in respect of the Premises.

(12) The Landlord notifies the Tenant in accordance with Section 48 of the Landlord and Tenant Act 1987 that his address for service is [insert address for service].

(13) If at any time the rent (or any part) is unpaid for 14 days after becoming due (whether or not formally demanded) or if any agreement or obligation on the Tenant's part is not complied with, or if any of the circumstances mentioned in Grounds 8, 10, or 11 to 15 of Part II of Schedule 2 to the

Housing Act 1988 shall arise, then the Landlord may re-enter the Premises and the tenancy shall be determined. This is to be without prejudice to any right of action the Landlord may have in respect of the Tenant's obligations under this Agreement. This right of re-entry is not to be exercised by the Landlord without a court order whilst anyone is residing in the Premises or whilst the tenancy is an assured tenancy.

(14) *Break clause*

1. The Landlord may terminate this tenancy at any time upon service on the Tenant of not less than 4 weeks' notice in writing expiring at any time if the Landlord:
   (a) requires the property for occupation by himself or any member of the Landlord's family; or
   (b) wishes to sell the property with vacant possession; or
   (c) has died and the Landlord's personal representatives require vacant possession either to sell the property or so that it can be occupied by a beneficiary under the Landlord's will or intestacy.

2. Where the Landlord for the time being comprises more than one person, references in this clause are to any one of them.

(15) The Landlord may increase the rent payable under this Agreement at any time during the tenancy by giving not less than 14 days' notice in writing prior to a rent payment day specifying the new rent. The Tenant will then pay the new rent on and from that rent payment date.

IN WITNESS the parties have signed this agreement as a deed on the date first mentioned.

Signed [landlord's signature] Landlord, in the presence of [witness' signature]

Signed [tenant's signature] Tenant, in the presence of [witness' signature]

INDEX

226

LE PORTRAIT DE M. DE RÊNAL, LIVRE I, CHAPITRE 1

DE « SI, EN ENTRANT À VERRIÈRES, LE VOYAGEUR DEMANDE À QUI APPARTIENT CETTE BELLE FABRIQUE DE CLOUS» À « SONT AUSSI LA RÉCOMPENSE DE LA SCIENCE DE M. DE RÊNAL DANS LE COMMERCE DU FER.»

Photo by kumweni on Unsplash

Dans un premier lieu le narrateur procède à une description physique de M. de Rênal : "un grand homme, il a un grand front, un nez aquilin, et au total sa figure ne manque pas d'une certaine régularité ". Puis, rapidement, le narrateur place M. de Rênal par rapport au village : " À son aspect tous les chapeaux se lèvent rapidement", "Tel est le maire de Verrières, M. de Rênal" et " Les murs en terrasse qui soutiennent les diverses parties de ce magnifique jardin, qui, d'étage en étage, descend jusqu'au Doubs". A travers les différents exemples cités il est facile de se rendre compte que M. de Rênal est un personnage central dans la vie du village, et que tous le respectent profondément. De plus il serait descendant d'une lignée espagnoles antique, et chevalier de plusieurs ordres : "Sa famille, dit-on, est espagnole, antique, et, à ce qu'on prétend, établie dans le pays bien avant la conquête de Louis XIV." et "Il est chevalier de plusieurs ordres". Cette généalogie est impossible à vérifier puisque trop ancienne, on peut donc se douter que M. de Rênal fabule sur ses origines afin de se construire une identité respectable.

Cependant, le voyageur parisien, étranger à ce village, perçoit rapidement les failles de ce personnage prétentieux : "Mais bientôt le voyageur parisien est choqué d'un certain air de contentement de soi et de suffisance mêlé à je ne sais quoi de borné et de peu inventif. On sent enfin que le talent de cet homme-là se borne à se faire payer bien exactement ce qu'on lui doit, et à payer lui-même le plus tard possible quand il doit."

Le premier à se rendre compte est éloigné de la situation et peut donc porter sur la ville un regard neuf, c'est le voyageur parisien. De plus certaines métaphores à la fin du texte appuient ces accusations : "Au-delà c'est une ligne d'horizon formée par les collines de la Bourgogne, et qui semble faite à

souhait pour le plaisir des yeux"
représentant l'incapacité des
campagnards à voir la supercherie,
"Les murs en terrasse qui
soutiennent les diverses parties de
ce magnifique jardin, qui, d'étage
en étage, descend jusqu'au Doubs"
qui représente le caractère supérieur
de M. de Rênal, mais qui reste
pourtant attaché aux bassesses du
monde. C'est donc le narrateur qui
se cache derrière le voyageur
parisien, afin que le lecteur prenne
conscience des sens cachés des
descriptions du paysage.

Chapitre 2

LA TYRANNIE DE L'OPINION, LIVRE I, CHAPITRE 1

DE « NE VOUS ATTENDEZ POINT À TROUVER EN FRANCE CES JARDINS PITTORESQUES» À «QU'AUX ETATS-UNIS D'AMÉRIQUE»

Photo by Jace & Afsoon on Unsplash

1. Une page d'exposition

2. La dictature de l'argent

3. Un discours violemment critique

I) Une page d'exposition

Tout d'abord, le récit peut-être perçu comme une page d'exposition, car le narrateur présente premièrement les lieux : "En Franche-Comté, plus on bâtit de murs, plus on hérisse sa propriété de pierres rangées les unes au-dessus des autres, plus on acquiert de droits aux respects de ses voisins." Il décrit également les caractéristiques de cette région et de ses habitants. Il énonce aussi quelques personnages principaux de son histoire, M. De Rênal : "M. le maire" et M. Sorel : "Malgré sa fierté, M. le maire a dû faire bien des démarches auprès du vieux Sorel, paysan dur et entêté". De plus il décrit l'histoire des personnages : "Les jardins de M. de Rênal, remplis de murs, sont encore admirés parce qu'il a acheté au poids de l'or certains petits morceaux de terrain qu'ils occupent." Le narrateur raconte le contexte dans lequel se déroule l'histoire : "Une fois, c'était un jour de dimanche, il y a quatre ans de cela, M. de Rênal, revenant de l'église en costume de maire, vit de loin le vieux Sorel, entouré de ses trois fils, sourire en le regardant. Ce sourire a porté un jour fatal dans l'âme de M. le maire, il pense depuis lors qu'il eût pu obtenir l'échange à meilleur marché." Le lecteur peut alors se familiariser avec les personnages et avec le contexte.

II) La dictature de l'argent

Dans cet extrait, l'argent a une grande importance : "plus on bâtit de murs, plus on hérisse sa propriété de pierres rangées les unes au-dessus des autres, plus on acquiert de droits aux respects de ses voisins." Les personnes qui ont les moyens de se faire construire une grande et belle maison sont immédiatement respectées : "Les jardins de M. de Rênal, remplis de murs, sont encore admirés parce qu'il a acheté au poids de l'or certains petits morceaux de terrain qu'ils occupent." Le jardin qui est censé accueillir des plantes et de la végétation est envahi de murs, pour montrer la richesse du propriétaire, ce qui en devient ridicule. Il faut donc exposer sa richesse publiquement si les habitants veulent obtenir de la considération. De plus la notion d'argent revient encore à plusieurs reprises dans cet extrait avec le champ lexical de la richesse : "de beaux louis d'or" , "riche", "une somme de 6000 F." La réputation compte également beaucoup pour les habitants : "Une telle innovation vaudrait à l'imprudent bâtisseur une éternelle réputation de mauvaise tête, et il serait à jamais perdu auprès des gens sages et modérés qui distribuent la considération en Franche-Comté." Le narrateur dépeint alors une population superficielle qui ne juge que par l'apparence et l'argent.

III) Un discours violemment critique

Cette situation d'exposition est en réalité un discours critique. Le narrateur décrit la société superficielle de son temps : "plus on hérisse sa propriété de pierres rangées les unes au-dessus des autres, plus on acquiert de droits aux respects de ses voisins", et également l'influence de l'argent sur les habitants de la ville. Les résidents obsédés par l'argent en deviennent ridicules : "Les jardins de M. de Rênal, remplis de murs, sont encore admirés parce qu'il a acheté au poids de l'or certains petits morceaux de terrain qu'ils occupent." Le jardin perd sa fonction principale pour devenir une exposition de richesse. De plus, le narrateur ne fait pas que raconter l'histoire mais il exprime son avis au lecteur avec le discours indirect libre : "Dans le fait, ces gens sages y exercent le plus ennuyeux despotisme", il se moque des provinciaux qui se comportent comme des petits rois : "c'est à cause de ce vilain mot que le séjour des petites villes est insupportable, pour qui a vécu dans cette grande république qu'on appelle Paris. La tyrannie de l'opinion, et quelle opinion ! est aussi bête dans les petites villes de France, qu'aux Etats-Unis d'Amérique". Il montre également la stupidité de la société tout en apparence. Il critique alors ouvertement la société provinciale où les habitants se croient haut placés et ne jurent que par leur richesse et leurs biens matériels au point d'en devenir ridicules.

Conclusion:

Ainsi, nous avons pu voir que cet extrait est alors une situation d'exposition, où le lecteur découvre les personnages la ville et la société dictée par l'argent et l'apparence. Mais aussi, une critique de la part du narrateur qui exprime son exaspération vis à vis de la société provinciale qu'il juge ridicule.

Chapitre 3

LA SCIERIE, LIVRE I, CHAPITRE 4

DE «EN APPROCHANT DE SON USINE, LE PÈRE SOREL APPELA JULIEN DE SA VOIX DE STENTOR» À «C'ÉTAIT CELUI DE TOUS QU'IL AFFECTIONNAIT LE PLUS, LE MÉMORIAL DE SAINTE-HÉLÈNE.»

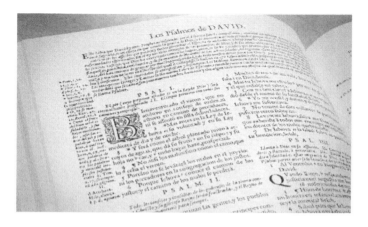

Photo by Marta Baena Simino on Unsplash

1. Une relation père-fils difficile et conflictuelle

2. L'importance du livre dans ce passage

3. Julien, un personnage romantique

I) Une relation père-fils difficile et conflictuelle

"En approchant de son usine, le père Sorel appela Julien de sa voix de stentor, personne ne répondit." : d'emblée le père est brutal envers son fils. Le père crie directement au lieu de parler, on voit qu'il veut réprimander Julien. Il n'y a pas d'amorce de communication. Julien ne répond pas à son propre père. Il semble être sourd à la voix de son père.

"Il ne vit que ses fils aînés, espèces de géants qui, armés de lourdes haches, équarrissaient les troncs de sapin, qu'ils allaient porter à la scie." : le père préfère ses fils aînés à Julien à cause de leur ressemblance physique.

"la terrible voix de son père" : le père est sévère et n'hésite pas à crier sur son fils ; il apparaît effrayant comme un ogre.

Le vieux Sorel se distingue par sa vivacité et sa brutalité qui contraste avec l'aspect fragile du jeune Julien : "malgré son âge, celui-ci sauta lestement sur l'arbre soumis à l'action de la scie" et "Un coup violent [...] un second coup aussi violent, donné sur la tête". : le père n'hésite pas à frapper son fils jusqu'à le mettre en danger.

"– Descends, animal, que je te parle." : inversion car c'est le père qui se comporte comme un animal : "et l'en frappa sur l'épaule", "le chassant rudement devant lui".

"– «Dieu sait ce qu'il va me faire !» se disait le jeune homme." : on voit que Julien a l'habitude d'être battu par son père.

II) L'importance du livre dans ce passage

"Il ne vit que ses fils aînés, espèces de géants qui, armés de lourdes haches, équarrissaient les troncs de sapin, qu'ils allaient porter à la scie." : Julien est différent des autres membres de sa famille qui sont représentés comme des barbares prêts à l'attaque.

"Tout occupés à suivre exactement la marque noire tracée sur la pièce de bois" : Julien n'écoute pas les ordres en choisissant de lire le livre ("il chercha vainement Julien à la place qu'il aurait dû occuper, à côté de la scie") alors que ses frères les suivent comme des moutons, ce qui montre un manque d'intelligence de leur part.

"Il l'aperçut à cinq ou six pieds plus haut, à cheval sur l'une des pièces de la toiture." : C'est une position symbolique; Julien est au-dessus des autres et le narrateur montre ainsi que ce personnage est plus intelligent que les autres car il désobéit.

"Au lieu de surveiller attentivement l'action de tout le mécanisme, Julien lisait." : détachement à droite après la virgule pour mettre en valeur l'action de lire par opposition au travail mécanique de la scierie.

"Rien n'était plus antipathique au vieux Sorel ; il eût peut-être pardonné à Julien sa taille mince peu propre aux travaux de force, et si différente de celle de ses aînés; mais cette manie de lecture lui était odieuse, il ne savait pas lire lui-même." : Le père souhaite que Julien soit comme ses frères et qu'il aide dans les travaux, même si son corps est moins puissant que les leurs. Il rejette tout ce qui est différent de lui dont la lecture, qu'il trouve être un vice. Le narrateur renforce le fait que le père est illettré en détachant cet aspect à droite de la phrase.

"L'attention que le jeune homme donnait à son livre bien plus que le bruit de la scie l'empêcha d'entendre la terrible voix de son père." : Julien est plus intéressé par son livre que par les travaux manuels que lui demande son père ; il est intellectuel.

"– Eh bien, paresseux ! tu liras donc toujours tes maudits livres, pendant que tu es de garde à la scie ? Lis-les le soir, quand tu vas perdre ton temps chez le curé, à la bonne heure." : Le père dénigre l'intelligence ainsi que la religion en précisant que ce sont des pertes de temps et en disant que les livres sont "maudits" alors qu'ils servent à s'élever. Julien va chez le curé pour apprendre le latin.

"pour la perte de son livre qu'il adorait.": pour Julien, le livre est plus important que tout le reste.

III) Julien, un personnage romantique

"Julien, quoi qu'étourdi par la force du coup, et tout sanglant, se rapprocha de son poste officiel, à côté de la scie." : registre pathétique. En lisant ce passage, le lecteur à de la compassion pour Julien tout "sanglant" par la main de son propre père et ainsi ressent de la pitié pour ce personnage.

"Il avait les larmes aux yeux, moins à cause de la douleur physique, que pour la perte de son livre qu'il adorait." : Le héros pleure montrant ainsi qu'il a du coeur. Il effectue ses actions avec du courage, même s'il a peur de son père. En latin coeur et courage ont la même racine.

"En passant, il regarda tristement le ruisseau où était tombé son livre ; c'était celui de tous qu'il affectionnait le plus, *Le Mémorial de Sainte-Hélène.*" : Julien est

passionné par l'empereur Napoléon
Ier.

Julien est isolé, mal à l'aise
dans sa famille. Comme tous les
héros romantiques, Julien ne se sent
pas adapté à la réalité. Il semble
souffrir de ce que Musset appellera
"le mal du siècle", un état
mélancolique voire dépressif. Julien
se réfugie dans les livres pour fuir
la réalité.

L'instruction est aussi un
moyen de fuir la pauvreté, grand
fléau du XIXème siècle. On a donc
aussi une critique sociale dans ce
passage.

Julien se caractérise par "sa taille mince, peu propre aux travaux de force" et "son air extrêmement pensif et sa grande pâleur" car le héros romantique est souvent maladif mais possède une grande force intérieure car l'âme et les sentiments ont pris le dessus sur le développement du corps.

Chapitre 4

LA PREMIÈRE RENCONTRE ENTRE JULIEN ET MADAME DE RÊNAL, LIVRE I CHAPITRE 6

DE «AVEC LA VIVACITÉ ET LA GRÂCE QUI LUI ÉTAIENT NATURELLES» À «QUOI, MONSIEUR, LUI DIT-ELLE ENFIN, VOUS SAVEZ LE LATIN ?»

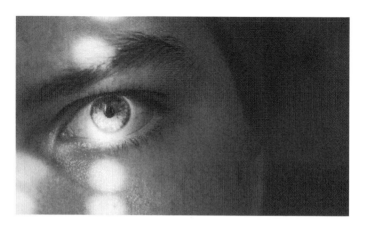

Photo by Matthias Oberholzer on Unsplash

1. Le point de vue de Julien
2. Le point de vue de Madame de Rênal

I) Le point de vue de Julien

Tout d'abord Julien est décrit comme timide, mais son amour pour Mme de Rênal chasse sa timidité et fait place au courage : "il oublia une partie de sa timidité." Julien est "frappé" et "étonné" par la beauté de son interlocutrice. Ces deux mots font référence au champ lexical du coup de foudre. Ensuite Julien regarde plein d'admiration madame de Rênal: "Julien n'avait jamais vu un être aussi bien vêtu et surtout une femme avec un teint si éblouissant". Il la trouve élégante. On peut remarquer le champ lexical du regard: "regard", "vu", "regarder".

On peut également observer que Julien la trouve particulièrement douce avec lui: "lui parler d'un air doux." Il en est touché car son père est très violent envers lui.

De plus Julien est tellement ébahi devant madame de Rênal qu'il oublie pourquoi il est là : "il oublia tout, même ce qu'il venait faire".

Malgré son amour pour Mme de Rênal, Julien reste très attentif à l'image qu'il renvoie, ce qui sera son trait de caractère principal dans tout le roman puisque c'est son orgueil qui causera sa perte : " tout honteux de ses larmes qu'il essuyait de son mieux".

II) Le point de vue de Madame de Rênal

Au premier regard Mme de Rênal prend Julien pour un paysan, elle remarque également que ce dernier a pleuré et est intimidé par elle : "quand elle aperçut près de la porte d'entrée la figure d'un jeune paysan presque encore enfant, extrêmement pâle et qui venait de pleurer". Mme de Rênal est donc attendrie par le jeune homme.

Ensuite on peut remarquer que Julien fait pitié à Mme de Rênal, cela le rend encore plus attachant: "Elle eut pitié de cette pauvre créature, arrêtée à la porte d'entrée, et qui évidemment n'osait pas lever la main jusqu'à la sonnette".

De plus elle le trouve enfantin mais également beau et charmant. Malgré tout madame de Rênal est séduire par Julien: "elle se moquait d'elle-même et ne pouvait se figurer tout son bonheur".

Elle est également surprise de voir qu'un jeune homme si doux et

si beau soit assez érudit pour être le précepteur de ses enfants : " –
Quoi, monsieur, lui dit-elle enfin, vous savez le latin ?"

Enfin on observe un passage au discours indirect libre qui nous donne accès aux pensées intimes du personnage : "Quoi, c'était là ce précepteur qu'elle s'était figuré comme un prêtre sale et mal vêtu, qui viendrait gronder et fouetter ses enfants !"

Chapitre 5

LA CONQUÊTE DE MME DE RÊNAL, LIVRE I, CHAPITRE 9

DE «ON S'ASSIT ENFIN, MADAME DE RÊNAL À CÔTÉ DE JULIEN, ET MADAME DERVILLE PRÈS DE SON AMIE.» À «IL S'ENFERMA À CLEF DANS SA CHAMBRE, ET SE LIVRA AVEC UN PLAISIR TOUT NOUVEAU À LA

LECTURE DES EXPLOITS DE SON HÉROS.»

Photo by Mihail Macri on Unsplash

1. Une scène d'amour
2. Un combat

I) Une scène d'amour

"On s'assit enfin, Mme de Rênal à côté de Julien, et Mme Derville près de son amie" : présentation des personnages, le positionnement de ceux-ci: Mme de Rênal est tiraillée entre Julien(amour interdit) et Mme Derville(vertu).

"Que de fois ne désira-t-il pas voir survenir à Mme de Rênal quelque affaire qui l'obligeât de rentrer à la maison et de quitter le jardin! : Il a peur que Madame de Rênal ne doive le quitter avant qu'il n'accomplisse son exploit.

"Bientôt la voix de Mme de Rênal devint tremblante aussi :

Madame de Rênal est réellement amoureuse de Julien.

"le dernier coup de dix heures retentissait": Julien est absorbé par le temps. Le dernier coup marque la fin de sa pensée. Il doit mettre en oeuvre son plan d'exécution.

"il étendit la main, et prit celle de mme de Rênal" : Par ce geste traditionnel, on voit que mme de Rênal éprouve des sentiments mais essaye de se maîtriser.

"sans trop savoir ce qu'il faisait" : Julien se laisse aller à ses sentiments qui ne sont pour une fois pas calculés.

"il fut frappé par la froideur glaciale de la main qu'il prenait" Julien pense que Mme de Rênal n'est pas d'accord avec sa décision et il a peur sa réaction.

"force convulsive" : le sentiment amoureux de Julien s'exprime.

II) Un combat

"On s'assit enfin, Mme de Rênal à côté de Julien, et Mme Derville près de son amie" : Mme de Rênal est considérée comme un objet qu'on se dispute.

"Préoccupé de ce qu'il allait tenter, Julien ne trouvait rien à dire": L'imparfait met l'emphase sur la durée de la pensée de Julien qui réfléchit sur son stratagème l.3 " la conversation languissait" Comme Julien est en train de réfléchir, il ne participe pas à la conversation donc celle-ci meurt (silence désagréable).

Julien pense aux futurs combats au lieu de penser à son amour. Nous avons des adjectifs qui caractérisent son état d'âme : il est tremblant de peur au lieu de joie et malheureux au lieu d'heureux. Ces deux adjectifs renvoient à sa lâcheté et à son égoïsme puisque le narrateur se focalise sur les sentiments de Julien. Madame de Rênal joue le rôle d'un objet que l'on essaye de s'approprier.

"il avait trop de méfiance et de lui et des autres, pour ne pas voir l'état de son âme" : Julien se livre un combat intérieur : il mène le combat sur 3 fronts contre lui-même, Madame de Rênal et Madame de Derville.

"Dans sa mortelle angoisse, tous les dangers lui eussent semblé préférables" : Nous apprenons la peur de Julien, il a tellement peur qu'il s'imagine dans la pire situation.

"Bientôt la voix de Mme de Rênal devint tremblante aussi, mais Julien ne s'en aperçut point". Julien t est tellement égoïste qu'il ne s'aperçoit pas qu'il a atteint son but.

"l'affreux combat que le devoir livrait à sa timidité était trop pénible": Dans cette scène amoureuse, Julien fait passer l'idée de son devoir avant celle de l'amour.

"Neuf heure trois quart venait de sonner à l'horloge du château sans qu'il eût rien encore osé" : Renvoie au récit de bataille avec a une heure précise le déplacement des troupes.

Julien se donne un objectif précis, "dix heures sonneront" : Le plan doit se mettre en marche.

Julien veut se suicider par orgueil et non pas par amour, c'est choquant.

"cette cloche fatale" : C'est le rythme du temps qui est fatal et non pas l'amour.

"retentissait dans sa poitrine" : Son cœur bat plus fort a cause de son angoisse que de son amour.

"mouvement physique" :
Julien ressent le temps, il a intégré
le rythme de la cloche.

"on fit un dernier effort pour la
lui ôter, mais enfin cette main lui
resta" : défaite de Mme de Rênal.

Chapitre 6

LA PASSION DE MADAME DE RÊNAL, LIVRE I, CHAPITRE 10

DE « TOUT À COUP L'AFFREUSE PAROLE : ADULTÈRE, LUI APPARUT» À « SANS S'EN DOUTER, MADAME DE RÊNAL JETA DES CRIS QUI RÉVEILLÈRENT SA FEMME DE CHAMBRE»

Photo by Gabriel Matula on Unsplash

1. Un dilemme tragique

2. Une héroïne tourmentée

I) Un dilemme tragique

     a)   L'origine du débat intérieur

Madame de Rênal commence à prendre conscience qu'elle est amoureuse de Julien Sorel, le jeune précepteur de ses enfants. Cele génère chez elle un sentiment violent de culpabilité : « Tout à coup l'affreuse parole : adultère, lui apparut ». Du coup elle se retrouve déchirée entre la force de son amour et le carcan des conventions sociales. Prise dans un affreux dilemme, elle va jusqu'à envisager d'avouer son amour pour Julien à son mari, ce qui serait une erreur fatale : « Elle eut un instant la pensée d'avouer à son mari qu'elle craignait d'aimer Julien. […] Heureusement elle rencontra dans sa mémoire un précepte donné jadis par sa tante, la veille de son mariage. Il s'agissait du danger des confidences faites à un mari, qui après tout est un maître. »

b) L'utilisation du discours rapporté

L'utilisation du discours indirect libre permet au lecteur d'entrer dans l'intimité des pensées du personnage et de partager sa souffrance : « Ce moment fut affreux ; son âme arrivait dans des pays inconnus. La veille elle avait goûté un bonheur inéprouvé ; maintenant elle se trouvait tout à coup plongée dans un malheur atroce. »

II) Une héroïne tourmentée

a) Les hyperboles

Le trouble du personnage se traduit par des pensées excessives « tantôt l'affreuse idée du crime la torturait comme si le lendemain elle eût dû être exposée au pilori, sur la place publique de Verrières, avec un écriteau expliquant son adultère à la populace ». Mais aussi par des gestes et des cris involontaires : « Sans s'en douter, madame de Rênal jeta des cris qui réveillèrent sa femme de chambre ».

b) La passion

Madame de Rênal est un personnage romantique, totalement

sous le joug de ses émotions qu'elle est incapable de contrôler : « Dans l'excès de sa douleur elle se tordait les mains. » Elle se comporte ici comme une héroïne de tragédie livrée entièrement à une passion violente qui lui fait perdre toute capacité de réflexion : « Elle n'avait aucune idée de telles souffrances, elles troublèrent sa raison ».

Chapitre 7

LA SCÈNE D'AMOUR, LIVRE I, CHAPITRE 15

DE «CE BRUIT LE RÉVEILLA COMME LE CHANT DU COQ RÉVEILLA SAINT PIERRE» À «CELUI D'UN HOMME ACCOUTUMÉ À ÊTRE BRILLANT AVEC LES FEMMES»

Photo by freestocks.org on Unsplash

1. Madame de Rênal, un personnage passionné et sincère

2. Julien, un hypocrite maladroit et peu courageux

I) Madame de Rênal, un personnage passionné et sincère

Tout d'abord, on nous présente la vertu de Madame de Rênal : "elle lui parlait avec une extrême dureté", "Mortellement effrayée". Au cours du texte, pour respecter la vertu du personnage, ainsi que son honneur, Stendhal a employé de nombreuses litotes afin de laisser le lecteur imaginer la scène d'amour sans qu'il n'ait à la décrire par respect pour Madame de Rênal: "il n'avait plus rien à désirer". La citation "Les pleurs et le désespoir de Julien la troublaient vivement" nous prouve que son amour pour Julien est sincère car elle est bouleversée. Mais la raison ne pouvait pas dépasser tout l'amour qu'elle avait pour lui: "Même, quand elle n'eut plus rien à lui refuser, elle repoussait Julien loin d'elle, avec une indignation réelle, et ensuite se jetait dans ses bras". Madame de Rênal est une femme très sensible, qui lutte contre sa passion, mais son amour est plus fort que sa vertu: "une sensibilité brûlante dans la femme qu'il venait d'enlever", "Le départ de Julien ne fit point cesser les transports qui l'agitaient malgré elle, et ses combats avec les remords qui la déchiraient".

II) Julien, un hypocrite maladroit et peu courageux

En revanche, Julien est tout le contraire du personnage de Madame de Rênal. Le narrateur le juge comme irresponsable et orgueilleux : "Il n'avait plus songé à sa proposition impertinente". Dès le début du texte, on nous montre qu'il n'est pas très courageux, aller chez sa bien-aimée est une épreuve pour lui car il se laisse dominer par la peur : "jamais il ne s'était imposé une contrainte plus pénible", " il était tellement tremblant que ses genoux se dérobaient sous lui", "souffrant plus mille fois que s'il eût marché à la mort", "Il ouvrit la porte d'une main tremblante et en faisant un bruit effroyable". Par peur de se confronter à Madame de Rênal, il allait même jusqu'à espérer que son mari soit éveillé, afin de rebrousser chemin : "Il alla écouter à la porte de M. de Rênal, dont il put distinguer le ronflement. Il en fut désolé. Il n'y avait donc plus de prétexte pour ne pas aller chez elle". Julien se comporte comme un enfant lorsqu'il est face à Madame de Rênal : "Il ne répondit à ses reproches qu'en se jetant à ses pieds, en embrassant ses genoux". Il se lamente constamment et n'est jamais satisfait de ce qu'il obtient : "ne pas plaire à une femme si charmante lui parut le plus grand des malheurs", "Mon Dieu ! être heureux, être aimé, n'est-ce que ça ?" Dans une phrase où l'on remarque aussi le champ lexical du combat, le narrateur le juge aussi comme maladroit : "une victoire à laquelle ne l'eût pas conduit toute son adresse si maladroite". Son hypocrisie est représentée avec: "jouer le rôle", "l'idée du devoir ne cessa jamais d'être présente à ses yeux". L'orgueil de ce personnage est tellement important ("victime d'un orgueil bizarre") qu'il ne cesse de se questionner, un rien le perturbe: "Il craignait un remords affreux et un ridicule éternel, s'il s'écartait du modèle idéal qu'il se proposait de suivre. En un mot, ce qui faisait de Julien un être supérieur fut précisément ce qui l'empêcha de goûter le bonheur qui se plaçait sous ses pas", "Telle fut la première pensée de Julien, en rentrant dans sa chambre. Il était dans cet état d'étonnement et de trouble inquiet où tombe l'âme qui vient d'obtenir ce qu'elle a longtemps désiré", "N'ai-je manqué à rien de ce que je me dois à moi-même ? Ai-je bien joué mon rôle ? Et quel rôle ? celui d'un homme accoutumé à être brillant avec les femmes". Pour conclure, on peut dire que Julien est un personnage victime de son orgueil, ce qui le mènera à sa perte.

Chapitre 8

LA SÉPARATION, CHAPITRE 19

DE «- VA-T'EN, LUI DIT TOUT À COUP MME DE RÊNAL, EN OUVRANT LES YEUX.» À « ELLE PROMIT, IL PARTIT, MAIS FUT RAPPELÉ AU BOUT DE DEUX JOURS.»

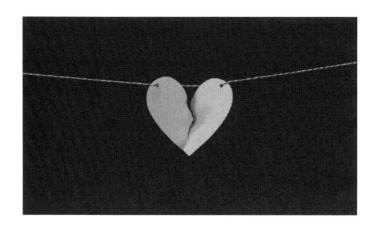

Photo by Kelly Sikkema on Unsplash

1. Le dilemme

2. La remise en cause involontaire du dilemme

3. La stratégie argumentative de Julien

I) Le dilemme

Les personnages de Madame
de Rênal et de Julien se croient
victimes de la colère de Dieu. Ils ne
savent pas quoi faire pour l'apaiser.
Madame de Rênal pleure jour et
nuit à cause de son fils Stanislas qui
est très malade. Surtout Madame de
Rênal croit que sa relation avec
Julien est un grand péché et que la
maladie de son fils est la punition
de Dieu pour son adultère. Or,
Julien à ce moment-là ne veut pas
la quitter: "Que deviendrai-je loin
de toi, et avec la conscience que tu
es malheureuse par moi! Mais qu'il
ne soit pas question de mes
souffrances. Je partirai, oui, mon
amour." Madame de Rênal est
complètement impuissante face à
l'amour qu'elle éprouve pour
Julien, mais reste cependant
rationnelle puisqu'elle sait qu'elle

n'arrivera jamais à aimer Julien comme un frère: "Et moi, s'écria-t-elle en se levant et prenant la tête de Julien entre ses deux mains, et la tenant devant ses yeux à distance, et moi, t'aimerai-je comme un frère? Est-il en mon pouvoir de t'aimer comme un frère?" La proposition de Julien de faire évoluer leur amour passionnel vers un amour fraternel est naïve et immature.

II) La remise en cause involontaire du dilemme

Après que Julien a souhaité être malade à la place de Stanislas, Madame de Rênal se jetant dans ses bras s'imagine une autre réalité dans laquelle son amour excessif (elle l'aime plus que son propre fils) pour Julien ne contrarierait pas Dieu: "Je te crois! je te crois! continua-t-elle, après s'être remise à genoux; ô mon unique ami! ô pourquoi n'es-tu pas le père de Stanislas? Alors ce ne serait pas un horrible péché de t'aimer mieux que ton fils."

III) La stratégie argumentative de Julien

Sans doute Julien a peur que Madame de Rênal afin de soulager sa souffrance raconte tout à son mari ce qui entraînerait et sa perte et celle de sa maîtresse. Il ne veut pas la laisser seule de peur qu'elle commette une erreur qui leur ferait du tort à tous les deux ainsi qu'à son mari : "Mais, si je te quitte, si je cesse de veiller sur toi, de me trouver sans cesse entre toi et ton mari, tu lui dis tout, tu te perds. Songe que c'est avec ignominie qu'il te chassera de sa maison;" Julien, qui ne voulait pas la quitter, propose une solution qui lui permettrait de rester près d'elle : "Veux-tu me permettre de rester, et que désormais je ne t'aime que comme un frère? C'est la seule expiation raisonnable, elle peut apaiser la colère du Très-Haut." Cependant les exagérations donnent l'impression que Julien met en scène sa propre souffrance, car il est avant tout pragmatique et veut préserver les apparences sociales : "Songe que je ne pourrai plus revenir si tu parles."

Chapitre 9

LE SÉMINAIRE, CHAPITRE 25

DE « IL VIT DE LOIN LA CROIX DE FER DORÉ SUR LA PORTE» À « C'EST LA VIOLENTE IMPRESSION DU LAID SUR UNE ÂME FAITE POUR AIMER CE QUI EST BEAU.»

Photo by malcolm lightbody on Unsplash

1. Le portrait d'un démon
2. Un séjour en enfer

I) Le portrait d'un démon

L'homme qui vient ouvrir la porte ressemble à un vampire: « un homme pâle, vêtu de noir ». Il fait peur à Julien : « Julien le regarda et

aussitôt baissa les yeux. » Il
ressemble à un démon, ce qui est
renforcé par l'image du chat,
animal associé aux sorcières, et à la
couleur verte qui est la couleur du
diable : « La pupille saillante et
verte de ses yeux s'arrondissait
comme celle d'un chat ». En effet,
dans la littérature les monstres et
les démons ont traditionnellement
les yeux verts car Lucifer portait
une émeraude au doigt lorsqu'il a
été chassé du paradis et précipité
dans les flammes de l'enfer.
L'homme montre par son attitude et
sa physionomie une absence totale
de sentiments : « les contours
immobiles de ses paupières
annonçaient l'impossibilité de toute
sympathie ; ses lèvres minces se
développaient en demi-cercle sur
des dents qui avançaient. » Julien

est un jeune homme romantique et passionné, il est donc terrorisé à l'idée de devenir insensible comme lui s'il reste dans ce lieu maléfique : « Cependant cette physionomie ne montrait pas le crime, mais plutôt cette insensibilité parfaite qui inspire bien plus de terreur à la jeunesse. »

II) Un séjour en enfer

« Voilà donc cet enfer sur la terre, dont je ne pourrai sortir ! » : le séminaire est un lieu privé de vie, austère et froid (même la croix sur la porte est en fer et non pas en bois), « Un silence de mort régnait dans toute la maison. » C'est un lieu d'enfermement et donc de solitude : « Le bruit de la cloche retentit comme dans un lieu solitaire. » La description du séminaire est digne du romantisme noir (cf. Le château d'Otrante d'Horace Walpole) : « Ils montèrent deux étages par un large escalier à rampe de bois, dont les marches déjetées penchaient tout à fait du côté opposé au mur, et semblaient prêtes à tomber. » La pièce dans laquelle l'effrayant homme en noir conduit Julien ressemble en tout point à un caveau de cimetière : « Une petite porte, surmontée d'une grande croix de cimetière en bois blanc peint en noir, fut ouverte avec difficulté, et le portier le fit entrer dans une chambre sombre et basse, dont les murs blanchis à la chaux étaient garnis de deux grands tableaux noircis par le temps. » Même le fauteuil ressemble à un cercueil : « un petit fauteuil en planches de sapin sans coussin ». Julien se retrouve ainsi confronté à l'image de sa propre mort : « L'émotion et la terreur de Julien étaient telles, qu'il lui semblait être sur le point de tomber. » Le séminaire est donc présenté comme un lieu où aucune forme de vie n'est possible, car pour Stendhal l'homme est fait pour l'amour et l'art : « C'est la violente impression du laid sur une âme faite pour aimer ce qui est beau. »

Chapitre 10

JULIEN INTERROGE SA DESTINÉE, LIVRE I, CHAPITRE 10

DE «JULIEN PRENAIT HALEINE UN INSTANT À L'OMBRE DE CES GRANDES ROCHES» À «C'ÉTAIT LA DESTINÉE DE NAPOLÉON, SERAIT-CE UN JOUR LA SIENNE ?»

Photo by Elijah Hiett on Unsplash

1. Un personnage ambitieux

2. Le paysage symbolique

I) Un personnage ambitieux

"Cette position physique le fit sourire, elle lui peignait la position qu'il brûlait d'atteindre au moral" : Le fait que cela le fasse sourire, montre qu'il a confiance en ses capacités et le désir ardent d'atteindre cette position sociale.

"mais Julien sentait que la haine qui venait de l'agiter, malgré la violence de ses mouvements, n'avait rien de personnel." : Julien ressent de la jalousie envers les personnes d'un rang social supérieur au sien.

Le champ lexical de la guerre : "sacrifice", "danger", "victoires", "mérite", "regardait le ciel, embrasé" montre que l'ascension sociale pour Julien s'apparente à un combat. "Mais à demain les pénibles recherches." : on dirait que Julien est éclaireur dans l'infanterie. En tant que grand admirateur de Napoléon 1er, Julien est un manipulateur qui réfléchit toujours en termes de stratégies et qui voit tous les autres personnages du roman comme des ennemis à vaincre, même les femmes dont il sera amoureux.

"Ses mouvements tranquilles et puissants le frappaient, il enviait cette force, il enviait cet isolement.

C'était la destinée de Napoléon, serait-ce un jour la sienne ?" : l'ambition de Julien est démesurée, dans cette question rhétorique, il se prend pour Napoléon ce qui le rend ridicule.

II) Le paysage symbolique

"Julien prenait haleine un instant à l'ombre de ces grandes roches, et puis se remettait à monter." : symboliquement cette phrase indique que Julien a commencé son ascension sociale bien qu'il soit encore "à l'ombre" des personnes riches et puissantes,

et notamment Monsieur de Rênal :
"Le maire de Verrières était bien
toujours, à ses yeux, le représentant
de tous les riches et de tous les
insolents de la terre".

"il se trouva debout sur un roc
immense et bien sûr d'être séparé
de tous les hommes" : le fait d'être
debout sur un rocher c'est un topos
romantique, et Julien se sent
différent des membres de sa famille
c'est pour cette raison qu'il est
représenté comme isolé et placé en
hauteur.

"L'air pur de ces montagnes
élevées communiqua la sérénité et
même la joie à son âme." : La

visualisation de son futur succès rend Julien serein et euphorique.

"Il voyait à ses pieds vingt lieues de pays" : Julien veut mettre le monde sous ses pieds.

"Quelque épervier parti des grandes roches au-dessus de sa tête était aperçu par lui, de temps à autre, décrivant en silence ses cercles immenses." : L'épervier représente Julien qui réfléchit à sa stratégie.

Chapitre 11

L'ENTRÉE DANS LE MONDE, LIVRE II, CHAPITRE 2

DE «JE VOUS RENDS VOTRE LIBERTÉ POUR DEUX JOURS» À «CE QUE LE MARQUIS DE LA MOLE VIENT DE FAIRE POUR MOI»

Photo by Augustin de Montesquiou on Unsplash

1. Un changement de destin

2. Les premières leçons parisiennes

I) Un changement de destin

Nous pouvons voir un changement de destin pour Julien grâce aux différents personnages dans cette scène. Nous avons le personnage de l'abbé qui semble douter et craindre l'avenir de Julien : "Si vous dites un mot, ils trouveront le secret de se moquer de vous." Puis il y a aussi le personnage du Marquis de La Mole qui veut aider Julien à entrer dans le monde : "M. de Rênal se serait cru déshonoré à jamais dans la centième partie de ce que le marquis de La Mole vient de faire pour moi." De plus, nous pouvons voir que l'attitude des deux hommes est très différente, l'abbé se place en figure d'autorité paternelle et donne des ordres à Julien : "Après-demain matin, ce tailleur vous portera deux habits ; vous donnerez cinq francs au garçon qui vous les essaiera", tandis que le Marquis est généreux et n'aime pas commander, "c'est un homme actif qui prévoit tout, et qui aime mieux faire que commander."

Le changement de destin dans cette scène est aussi relevé grâce à l'opposition entre Paris et la province. Nous pouvons voir que le narrateur emploie de l'ironie pour souligner la différence entre la province et Paris : "le bon abbé était trop provincial lui-même pour voir que Julien avait encore cette démarche des épaules, qui en province est à la fois élégance et importance." Cette différence souligne donc une opposition entre les deux hommes qui souhaitent aider Julien.

II) Les premières leçons parisiennes

Julien apprend ses premières leçons parisiennes dans cet extrait. Nous pouvons tout d'abord voir que l'abbé dit à Julien de se méfier de ces "Parisiens-là", expression qui est péjorative. Cette méfiance et cette crainte de l'abbé sont confirmées quelques paragraphes plus bas, lorsque Julien se fait voler sa montre à Paris, "Mais en se séparant de ce libéral, qui, les larmes aux yeux, le serrait presque dans ses bras, Julien n'avait plus de montre." Encore une fois, le narrateur emploie de l'ironie pour se moquer du personnage de Julien, qui est un jeune homme naïf et nouveau à Paris. Nous pouvons aussi voir qu'à Paris, l'apparence est très importante et très valorisée, comme nous le dit le marquis de la Mole, "prenez encore vingt-deux chemises." A la fin de cet extrait, Julien est épaté par ce que le marquis de la Mole lui montre, le jardin immense et la bibliothèque magnifique avec des beaux livres. Mais cette idée de Paris que se fait Julien est superficielle, car en réalité, Paris est une ville remplie d'escrocs et de pièges. Nous pouvons donc voir grâce à cela que

nous sommes dans un roman
d'apprentissage, ce qui laisse
imaginer que Julien devra
surmonter de nombreuses épreuves
en raison de sa trop grande naïveté.

Chapitre 12

LA CONQUÊTE DE MATHILDE, LIVRE II, CHAPITRE 19

DE « PLUSIEURS FOIS L'IDÉE DU SUICIDE S'OFFRIT À LUI» À «QUI POURRA DÉCRIRE L'EXCÈS DU BONHEUR DE JULIEN ? CELUI DE MATHILDE FUT PRESQUE ÉGAL.»

Photo by Roksolana Zasiadko on Unsplash

1. L'intimité entre le narrateur et son personnage

2. La dramatisation du récit

3. La distance critique du narrateur par rapport à son personnage

I) L'intimité entre le narrateur et son personnage

– «Ma mort augmentera le
mépris qu'elle a pour moi ! s'écria-t-
il. Quel souvenir je laisserai !»:
Cette phrase nous montre l'intimité
entre le narrateur et son personnage
car le narrateur rentre dans les
pensées du héros.

– «Puis-je être plus
malheureux !» se disait-il.: Le
narrateur omniscient assiste à
l'évolution des pensées de Julien
qui se morfond sans véritable
raison.

– «Elle va se fâcher,
m'accabler de mépris, qu'importe ?
Je lui donne un baiser, un dernier
baiser, je monte chez moi et je me
tue...; mes lèvres toucheront sa joue

avant que de mourir !»: Dans ce passage le narrateur nous montre que Julien est très sentimental et très romanesque. Le narrateur retranscrit les pensées du personnage sans transition.

"Qui pourra décrire l'excès du bonheur de Julien ? celui de Mathilde fut presque égal.": Ceci montre que le narrateur est dans les pensées des deux personnages car il pose une question rhétorique, dont il sait déjà comment se sentent les deux personnages.

II) La dramatisation du récit

"Plusieurs fois l'idée du suicide s'offrit à lui, cette image était pleine de charmes, c'était comme un repos délicieux, c'était le verre d'eau glacée offert au misérable qui, dans le désert, meurt de soif et de chaleur." : Cette phrase nous montre la dramatisation du récit car il compare le suicide avec un repos délicieux, ou comme un verre d'eau, ce qui semble très dramatique. Cette pensée de Julien est très exagérée par rapport à la situation qu'il est en train de vivre puisque le motif qui causerait sa mort est un simple refus de recevoir un baiser sur la joue. C'est une parodie de la scène du balcon dans Roméo et Juliette de Shakespeare.

–"«Puis-je être plus malheureux !» se disait-il.": Julien exagère la situation, car il pourrait vivre des malheurs plus grands que de ne pas donner un baiser sur la joue de Mathilde.

"Il courut à l'échelle, le jardinier l'avait enchaînée. A l'aide du chien d'un de ses petits pistolets, qu'il brisa, Julien animé dans ce moment d'une force surhumaine, tordit un des chaînons de la chaîne qui retenait l'échelle ; il en fut maître en peu de minutes, et la plaça contre la fenêtre de Mathilde.": Le narrateur dramatise la situation en enchaînant une succession d'actions rapides et en montrant que Julien est confronté à des difficultés qu'il doit résoudre en se montrant "héroïque".

"elle veut ouvrir la persienne, l'échelle s'y oppose : Julien se cramponne au crochet de fer destiné à tenir la persienne ouverte, et, au risque de se précipiter mille fois, donne une violente secousse à l'échelle et la déplace un peu. Mathilde peut ouvrir la persienne." : La dramatisation du récit est présente dans cette phrase car un simple devoir semble être très dur pour Julien. Le narrateur utilise des mots comme "cramponne" et "violente" ce qui nous donne l'impression que Julien fait quelque chose de très difficile. Mais aussi, cela montre que Julien est très maladroit et impulsif car si

Mathilde ouvre les volets, elle fait tomber l'échelle, donc Julien n'a pas du tout réfléchi à ce qu'il a fait. La rapidité des actions est soulignée par le passage au présent de l'indicatif.

"C'est donc toi ! dit-elle en se précipitant dans ses bras." : Le narrateur dramatise ironiquement la situation en faisant en sorte que Mathilde est supérieure à Julien et qu'elle a plus de force que lui.

III) La distance critique du narrateur par rapport à son personnage

Julien est présenté comme un personnage très orgueilleux qui se soucie plus de sa réputation que de son amour pour lequel il dit pourtant risquer sa vie : "Quel souvenir je laisserai !".

Julien est un personnage calculateur puisqu'il passe son temps à imaginer ce que Mathilde pense et comment il pourrait la manipuler : "Ma mort augmentera le mépris qu'elle a pour moi !"

"Tombé dans ce dernier abîme du malheur, un être humain n'a de ressource que le courage.": Ce passage nous montre la critique du narrateur par rapport à son personnage car il fait un commentaire qui ridiculise son héros, mais cela montre aussi que le narrateur est omniscient.

Julien n'eut pas assez de génie pour se dire : – «Il faut oser» : Encore une fois le narrateur ridiculise son personnage, ici il critique le fait que son héros n'a pas de courage, et pas d'intelligence non plus. D'ailleurs, Julien est également dépourvu d'imagination : "il se figurait cette chambre charmante qu'il avait vue, hélas ! une fois en sa vie. Son imagination n'allait pas plus loin.", la déception du narrateur à l'égard du héros est soulignée par "hélas !".

"Ce fut l'éclair du génie" : Le narrateur critique encore une fois l'intelligence de son personnage car il ne faut pas grand chose pour prendre une échelle pour grimper à la fenêtre de quelqu'un.

"Julien animé dans ce moment d'une force surhumaine" : Le narrateur ridiculise son personnage présenté comme un héros de pacotille tout juste capable de détacher une échelle : "il en fut maître en peu de minutes".

Le narrateur nous transmet son affection pour son héros tout en s'amusant de sa maladresse : "Il se jette dans la chambre plus mort que vif" : Le narrateur se moque de la

fragilité de Julien, épuisé après
avoir réussi à entrer dans la
chambre de Mathilde.

Chapitre 13

JULIEN TIRE SUR MADAME DE RÊNAL, LIVRE II, CHAPITRE 35

DE «IL ARRIVA À VERRIÈRES UN DIMANCHE MATIN» À «IL TIRA UN SECOND COUP, ELLE TOMBA»

Photo by Tavis Beck on Unsplash

1. La dramatisation de la scène

2. Un suicide symbolique

I) La dramatisation de la scène

"Il arriva à Verrières un dimanche matin." : l'action se met en place de façon précise.

"Il entra chez l'armurier du pays, qui l'accabla de compliments sur sa récente fortune." : on voit l'ironie de Stendhal qui souligne le fait que le rêve de Julien lui glisse entre les doigts au moment même où il croyait l'atteindre. Il a eu la chance d'être anobli après la réussite de son stratagème pour épouser Mathilde et la lettre de délation de madame de Rênal va tout faire échouer.

"C'était la nouvelle du pays." : sa renommée va se retourner contre lui puisqu'il va se trouver en situation d'échec total à cause de la lettre.

"Les trois coups sonnaient" : comme au théâtre avant le lever du rideau, "Toutes les fenêtres hautes de l'édifice étaient voilées avec des rideaux cramoisis" : l'église devient le théâtre de l'action ce qui est doublement sacrilège puisque Julien va commettre un crime pendant la messe alors qu'en plus il a fait le séminaire.

"il tira sur elle un coup de pistolet et la manqua ; il tira un second coup, elle tomba.": le narrateur crée un effet de suspens avec l'action qui se passe en deux temps et la pause marquée par le point virgule.

II) Un suicide symbolique

"Julien eut beaucoup de peine à lui faire comprendre qu'il voulait une paire de pistolets." : Julien demande une paire de pistolets comme pour un duel alors qu'il va en fait se battre contre lui-même puisque son amour pour madame de Rênal lui fera manquer le premier coup.

"L'armurier sur sa demande chargea les pistolets." : Julien demande à l'armurier de charger les pistolets car il ne sait pas comment le faire.

"La vue de cette femme qui l'avait tant aimé fit trembler le bras de Julien d'une telle façon, qu'il ne put d'abord exécuter son dessein. Je ne le puis, se disait-il à lui-même ; physiquement, je ne le puis." : son amour pour madame de Rênal est si fort que lorsqu'il va tirer sur elle il aura le sentiment de tirer sur lui-même, sur sa moitié, son âme soeur.

"Julien ne la reconnaissait plus aussi bien" : il a besoin de se donner du courage car il n'arrive pas à tirer sur cette femme qu'il aime tant.

"il tira sur elle un coup de pistolet et la manqua ; il tira un second coup, elle tomba." : Julien est vraiment un anti-héros dans ce passage puisque même à quelques pas d'elle il n'arrive pas à la toucher du premier coup. Ses émotions le poussent vers l'échec dans l'ensemble du roman ce qui l'amène à ce suicide symbolique puisqu'en tirant sur madame de Rênal non seulement il perd sa raison de vivre inavouée mais il sait qu'il va être condamné à mort.

Chapitre 14

LA LETTRE DE MME DE RÊNAL AUX JURÉS, LIVRE II, CHAPITRE 40

DE «MALGRÉ TOUTES LES PROMESSES DE PRUDENCE FAITES AU DIRECTEUR DE SA CONSCIENCE ET À SON MARI» À «ET VOUS N'AUREZ PAS À VOUS REPROCHER LE SANG D'UN INNOCENT »

Photo by Debby Hudson on Unsplash

Mme de Rênal commence son argumentation en affirmant que la société n'a pas le droit d'arracher la vie à quelqu'un et surtout celle de Julien, "Non, sans doute, la société n'a point le droit d'arracher la vie, et surtout à un être tel que Julien Sorel" car il a des talents uniques : "quel est celui qui met en doute ses admirables talents et sa science profonde ?" Julien par ses démonstrations d'intelligence suscite la jalousie chez les personnes influentes : "Ce pauvre jeune homme a des ennemis puissants". Madame de Rênal met en avance son côté maternel en disant qu'elle lui a confié ses deux enfants et qu'ils ont été très bien éduqué. Le métier même de précepteur est honorable et Julien a confirmé tout cela par sa piété et sagacité: "Durant près de dix-huit mois, nous l'avons tous connu pieux, sage, appliqué". De plus elle mentionne les crises de nerfs dont Julien souffrait : "deux ou trois fois par an, il était saisi par des accès de mélancolie qui allaient jusqu'à l'égarement." Par ses arguments madame de Rênal veut plaider la folie de Julien pour qu'il soit déclaré irresponsable de ses actes. Elle invoque des témoins qui pourront plaider pour la cause de Julien en corroborant ses propos: "Toute la ville de Verrières, tous nos voisins de Vergy où nous passons la belle saison, ma famille entière, M. le sous-préfet lui-même, rendront justice à sa piété exemplaire". Madame de Rênal est prête à faire témoigner ses propres ses enfants pour essayer de sauver Julien : "Mes fils auront l'honneur de vous présenter cette lettre : ce sont des enfants. Daignez les interroger, monsieur, ils vous donneront sur ce pauvre jeune homme tous les détails qui seraient encore nécessaires pour vous convaincre de la barbarie qu'il y aurait à le condamner." Son amour l'aveugle à tel point qu'elle minimise l'acte de Julien en disant que la blessure a été très légère : "La blessure, qui a été le résultat d'un de ces moments de folie que mes enfants eux-mêmes remarquaient chez leur précepteur, est tellement peu dangereuse, qu'après moins de deux mois elle m'a permis de venir en poste de Verrières à Besançon." Elle est prête même à s'humilier devant le tribunal si sa démarche pouvait sauver Julien : "Si j'apprends, monsieur, que vous hésitiez le moins du monde à soustraire à la barbarie des lois un être si peu coupable, je sortirai de mon lit où me retiennent uniquement les ordres de mon mari et j'irai me jeter à vos pieds." Enfin Le personnage de Madame de Rênal veut culpabiliser les jurés en faisant planer sa propre mort et en lui imputant la mort d'un innocent : "N'en doutez point, l'affreuse idée qu'à cause de moi un innocent a été conduit à la mort empoisonnerait le reste de ma vie et sans doute l'abrégerait." et "Déclarez, monsieur, que la préméditation n'est pas constante, et vous n'aurez pas à vous reprocher le sang d'un innocent".

Madame de Rênal se donne toutes les peines pour aider Julien à s'en sortir, elle n'exclut aucune possibilité pour faire annuler la condamnation à mort de son amant. Elle veut même utiliser sa famille pour innocenter Julien. Stendhal, en fin théoricien de l'amour, joue avec ses personnages pour nous montrer jusqu'où l'amour peut nous mener.

Chapitre 15

EXCIPIT, LIVRE II, CHAPITRE 45

DE «LE MAUVAIS AIR DU CACHOT DEVENAIT INSUPPORTABLE À JULIEN» À «ELLE MOURUT EN EMBRASSANT SES ENFANTS.»

Photo by Josiah Ingels on Unsplash

1. Les intentions du dénouement
2. La mort du héros

I) Les intentions du dénouement

      Suite à la mort de Julien le récit continue : "si tu sais t'y prendre, ils te vendront ma dépouille mortelle... Fouqué réussit dans cette triste négociation", sa mort n'est même pas signalée, elle est insinuée :"auprès du corps de son ami", "ce qui reste de Julien". À la suite de sa mort, Fouqué et Mathilde vont aller enterrer Julien dans une grotte. Nous apprenons que Mme de Rênal meurt peu après Julien. En effet si le récit continue après la mort de Julien c'est pour clore l'histoire des autres personnages ce qui souligne leur importance et crée un contraste avec l'orgueil de Julien.

Fouqué est le meilleur ami de Julien, malgré toutes les erreurs et les défauts de Julien il lui restera fidèle jusqu'au bout. En effet Fouqué écoute et obéit silencieusement à Julien qui reste insensible face à la tristesse de son ami. Il lui demande de se faire enterrer dans une grotte et de faire mettre Mme de Rênal et Mathilde dans la même voiture. Fouqué lui, est meurtri de chagrin suite à la mort de son ami : "Il passait la nuit seul dans sa chambre, auprès du corps de son ami," Il est seul, il n'a même plus "le courage de parler ni de se lever". De plus il est même dit qu'il "faillit en devenir fou de douleur" ce qui relève du registre pathétique.

Mathilde, qui, pendant tout le roman est le miroir de Julien en terme d'orgueil et de romantisme va se balader avec la tête de son amant défunt ce qui est particulièrement macabre:"elle porta sur ses genoux la tête de l'homme" elle se comporte comme une héroïne tragique. Transportée par son orgueil elle est au "milieu" de la cérémonie d'enterrement c'est elle qui " voulut ensevelir de ses propres mains la tête de son amant." elle veut être le centre d'attention pour l'enterrement de son amant: elle a fait orne la grotte de marbre italien, elle a fait venir vingt prêtres pour l'enterrement et elle"fit jeter plusieurs milliers de pièces de cinq francs". De plus Mathilde tente de reproduire l'enterrement de son ancêtre: "Boniface de La Mole" ce qui la lie à un destin familial et renforce le caractère tragique de cet excipit.

Le personnage de Mme de Rênal relève lui aussi du tragique car on apprend qu'elle a tenu la promesse que lui à fait faire Julien. Cette promesse qui l'engageait à s'occuper de l'enfant que Julien a eu avec une autre maîtresse, Mathilde. Non seulement à t-elle tenu cette promesse malgré sa douleur mais elle va aussi mourir de ce chagrin, ce qui fait d'elle aussi une héroïne tragique.

II) La mort du héros

À L'approche de la mort Julien est présenté comme un romantique en connexion avec la nature, il ne ressentira pas de peur face à la mort : "mais de la peur, non on ne me verra point pâlir" De plus ce qui va accentuer l'aspect romantique de ce personnage est son choix d'enterrement, dans une grotte qui lui rappelle son ambition passée. En effet c'est depuis la vue que l'on à sur cette montagne que Julien à ressenti que "l'ambition a enflammé mon cœur". Malgré le caractère romantique de Julien dans ce dénouement il se montre insensible face à la douleur de son meilleur ami. Après lui avoir demandé plusieurs services, dans les derniers moments passés avec son meilleur ami il se plaint de l'état du cachot : "ce cachot si laid, si humide, me donne des moments de fièvre où je ne me reconnais pas". Et, toujours insensible à son ami, Julien va se montrer courageux pour satisfaire son orgueil quand il dit qu'il ne ressentira pas de peur face à la mort. Il donne plus d'importance à son orgueil qu'à son meilleur ami si proche de la mort, c'est peut être une manière pour Julien de mettre derrière lui son bonheur et de faire face à la réalité qui est celle de son exécution imminente. Une fois de plus c'est l'orgueil qui dicte sa conduite à Julien.

De plus nous pouvons dire que la mort de Julien donne du sens à sa destinée car il a toujours été très ambitieux mais il n'a jamais rien réussi de sa vie à part faire souffrir les gens qui l'aimaient. Ainsi sa mort met un terme à une longue série d'erreurs et Julien apparaît donc plus comme un anti-héros que comme un véritable héros puisqu'il n'a pas tiré les leçons de ses échecs tout au long de ce roman d'apprentissage.

Personnage

→ M. De Renal

→ Julien

Printed in Germany
by Amazon Distribution
GmbH, Leipzig

17909530R00070